SÈVRES

SÈVRES

Porcelain from the Sèvres Museum
1740 to the Present Day

Marie-Noëlle Pinot de Villechenon
Curator at the Sèvres Museum

Translated by John Gilbert

Lund Humphries Publishers · London

This English-language edition first published in 1997 by
Lund Humphries Publishers Ltd
Park House
1 Russell Gardens
London NW11 9NN

Originally published in France by
Réunion des Musées Nationaux, Paris, in 1993
as *Sèvres: Une collection de porcelaines 1740-1992*

Original French-language edition
© 1993 Réunion des Musées Nationaux

Sèvres: Porcelain from the Sèvres Museum 1740 to the Present Day
© 1997 Lund Humphries Publishers Ltd

British Library Cataloguing in Publication Data
A catalogue record for this book is available from
the British Library.

ISBN 0 85331 689 9

Designed by Jean-Yves Cousseau
Typeset by Nene Phototypesetters, Northampton
Printed by Midas Printing Limited in Hong Kong

Distributed in the USA by
Antique Collectors' Club
Market Street Industrial Park
Wappingers Falls
NY 12590
USA

PHOTOGRAPHIC CREDITS
Réunion des Musées Nationaux
(Martine Beck-Coppola, Christian Jean)

ACKNOWLEDGEMENTS
My thanks go in particular to Catherine Monnier,
researcher, Guy Sarrauste de Menthière, head of
conservation, and all the staff at the museum,
especially Christian Borgoltz and Sylvie Elbaz.

JACKET:
Details of the Bertin vase with elephant heads
1873
Pâte sur pâte decoration by Gély
(MNC 7,529²)

Contents

History of a Royal Porcelain Factory: From Vincennes to Sèvres

The Earliest Wares of the Vincennes Factory: 1740-1756

THE COLLECTIONS in the French National Museum of Ceramics (the Sèvres Museum) cannot be fully appreciated without some insight into the history and background of *porcelain** manufacture in France. The 5000 or so objects in the museum, ranging from modest ornaments to elaborate dinner services, are the fruit of a remarkable venture of research and experiment, conducted by craftsmen known as *arcanists:** men who possessed secret knowledge of the recipe for manufacturing porcelain.

During the reign of Louis XIV and under the Regency, porcelain factories, seeking to imitate the style which had recently been perfected in Saxony, sprang up successively, notably in the Île-de-France: at Saint-Cloud (in the 1670s), at Chantilly in 1725, at Mennecy in 1735, then at Vincennes in 1740 and finally at Sceaux in 1748. They found eager patrons among royalty and the aristocracy. Vincennes, from its earliest years, enjoyed royal protection, at first unofficially, later publicly.

In Saxony, the white clay known as *kaolin,** discovered in 1709, was recognised as the essential element for manufacturing porcelain in the traditional Chinese manner. The joint investigations of Johann Friedrich Böttger and Ehrenfried Walter von Tschirnhaus, in the service of Augustus the Strong, Prince-Elector of Saxony, culminated in 1710 in the establishment at Meissen of the first *hard-paste porcelain** factory in Europe.

In France, where kaolin was not yet known, the arcanists prepared a ceramic body based on white marl with the addition of frit, a glassy substance composed of silica, soda and alum. Other ingredients such as green soap and parchment glue, already fired, designed to give this body plasticity, were mixed and fired a second time with the frit at around 1250 degrees centigrade. The finished body, whose glaze is notable for its lead content, showed scratch marks when scored by metal, and was thus called *soft-paste porcelain.**

Around 1740 four former employees of Chantilly, the brothers Robert and Gilles Dubois, Louis-François Gravant and Claude-Humbert Gérin approached the aristocrat Orry de Fulvy, whose brother, Orry de Vignory,

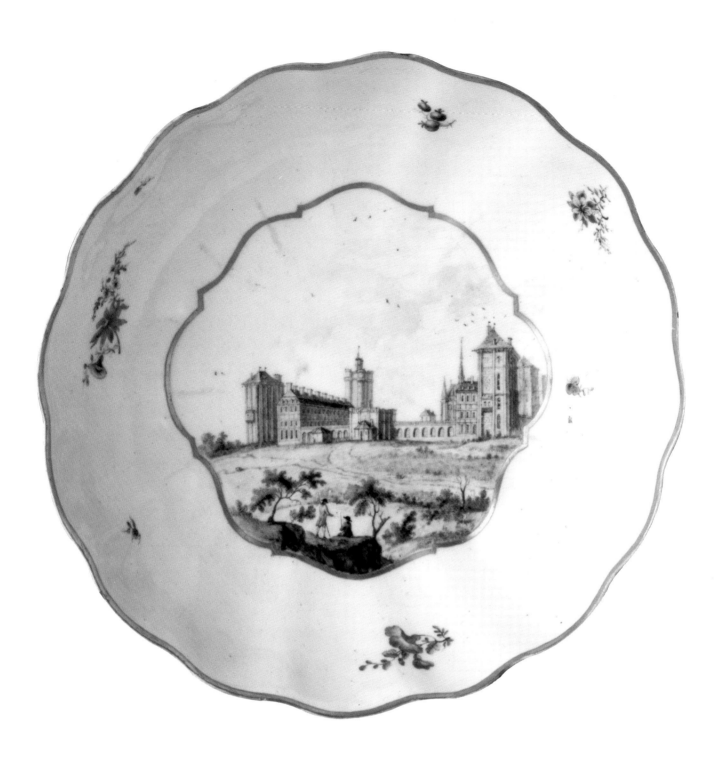

1.

*Dish showing the
Château of Vincennes*

Soft-paste porcelain
*c.*1749-53
H. 7 cm; D. 24 cm
Beurdeley Donation,
1846
(MNC 3,657)

Perhaps from a drawing by
Étienne Le Guay, itself based on
a print by Israël Silvestre. This
miniature version still imitates
the style of the Meissen factory
in Saxony.

was Minister of Finance. They were given the necessary encouragement and funds to open a porcelain factory in disused buildings at the Château of Vincennes (Plate 1). De Fulvy advanced the capital, and after 1745, Vincennes received additional support from the new Minister of Finance, Machault d'Arnouville.

According to rumour, however, it was the influential new favourite of King Louis XV (Plate 2), Jeanne Antoinette Le Normand d'Etiolles, the future Marquise de Pompadour (Plate 3), who helped determine the financial fortunes of Vincennes in those early years.

A decree of the Council of State of 25 July 1745 granted to the company that bore the name of Charles Adam (Orry de Fulvy's *valet de chambre*), the exclusive right for twenty years 'to manufacture porcelain in the Saxon manner, painted with human figures and gilded'. The shareholders were friends of Fulvy, almost all of them from the world of finance, including François de Verdun de Monchiroux and Antoine-Augustin Bouillard.

From that year of 1745 there appeared on the reverse of pieces made at Vincennes the double monogram of Louis XV: two Ls painted in blue with or without a dot inside. The mark designed on the *rocaille**-style container of the Vincennes bouquets of artificial flowers was particularly decorative, the two interlaced Ls being supplemented by a garland of leaves. ▲

In the course of the following years, although financial difficulties were never overcome, the factory continued to make steady progress, both technically and artistically. Gravant had pioneered the production of a usable soft-paste porcelain body at Vincennes and Gérin was later instrumental in resolving the problems of firing and improving the quality of the body. From 1748 onwards, the firing of a greatly expanded range of colours, and of gold, proved excellent.

The king, increasingly interested in porcelain manufacture, expressed a wish to transfer the factory to a place nearer to Versailles. The purchase of a site on the northern side of Sèvres, neighbouring Meudon, took place in March 1752.

The Charles Adam company was disbanded after paying

2.
Bust of Louis XV in armour

Soft-paste biscuit porcelain
1760
H. 41 cm
After J.-B. Lemoyne
(MNC 20,056)

Had Louis XV not agreed to give the Vincennes-Sèvres factory considerable help, this bust would never have been made public.

3.
Madame de Pompadour as goddess of friendship, also known as *Friendship*

Soft-paste biscuit porcelain
1755
H. 26.5 cm; L. 14 cm
Étienne Falconet
(MNC 16,057)

For some years the Marquise de Pompadour had no longer been the first royal favourite. Compelled to play the role of mistress and muse, she managed to interest the king in the Vincennes factory.

4.

Plate showing the main façade of the Sèvres factory

Hard-paste porcelain
1822
D. 24 cm
Gift of the Friends of the
Sèvres Museum, 1934
(MNC 18,701)

A work by the architect Lindet and the engineer Perronet in 1753 and 1756. These buildings were occupied by the factory from 1756 to 1876.

5.

Bouillard cup and saucer

Soft-paste porcelain
*c.*1749-50
Cup: H. 6.5 cm; D. 6.6 cm
Saucer: H. 2.5 cm; D. 12.5 cm
(MNC 26,470¹⁻²)

Harbour scenes, framed in gold with flowers scattered all around, were copies of the Meissen style, as was the mark of two crossed swords, but topped by the fleur de lys.

off all the shareholders: its successor, in 1753, consisting of more members, took the name of one Éloi Brichard.

Towards the end of that summer there appeared, along with the mark of two interlaced Ls, the first letter-date A, as seen under the oblong dish of the *service de Louis XV* (Plate 18). ▲ Each letter of the alphabet was added in due course until 1778, the date when the double letter sequence AA, BB, etc. was introduced, up to PP at the end of 1792. The mark that appears beneath the plate of the *service dit de Buffon* (Plate 40) bears the double letter GG, signifying that the object was finished between the summer of 1784 and the summer of 1785.

In 1754 the Éloi Brichard company appealed for new funds to pay for the Sèvres factory, built by the architect Lindet, under the direction of the engineer Jean-Rodolphe Perronet. The buildings of the new factory (Plate 4) were completed at Sèvres in mid-1756. The move evidently went smoothly, as the first kiln was installed in August of that year. The factory was to occupy this magnificent eighteenth-century building until 1876. Eventually, in autumn 1759, Louis XV bought up all the shares. The factory then saw its best years from 1759 until 1772 under the direction of Jacques-René Boileau.

During that time, a surgeon named Darnet, from Saint-Yrieix, south of Limoges, made a discovery near the town of a deposit of white clay which his apothecary colleague from Bordeaux, M. Villaris, identified as kaolin.

Meanwhile, Pierre-Joseph Macquer, a chemist and member of the Academy of Sciences, had been working at Sèvres to discover the secret of hard-paste porcelain. For two years he had carried out experiments every bit as complex as those undertaken by the arcanists in the early part of the century. Eventually, on 28 October 1768, Macquer, having travelled far and wide with Robert Millot, head of the kilns, was informed by Villaris of the existence of the clays of Saint-Yrieix. Soon afterwards he wrote to his brother: 'The new clay is so white and so beautiful that you have to kneel before it.' The manufacture of hard-paste porcelain is, in fact, far simpler than that of soft-paste porcelain. As its name suggests, it is stronger and will not show metal scratch marks.

6.

Bouquet of flowers in a jardinière

Soft-paste porcelain
*c.*1750-1
H. total with bouquet: 56 cm
(MNC 25,058)

Flowers were the first major
success for the Vincennes factory.
They were comparatively easy to
produce and fire. The *jardinière* or
jatte has *rocaille* decoration, fairly
typical of Duplessis' designs.

The first wares made at Vincennes during its earliest years were modelled on the designs of the Meissen factory. Initially, insects and flowers were scattered over the surface in an awkwardly random manner but were eventually grouped together to form a more harmonious pattern. Similarly, rustic or picturesque scenes (Plate 5), framed by gilt scrolls, depicted small Watteau-type figures.

Porcelain flowers (Plate 6) were produced from about 1741 onwards, and between 1745 and 1750 Vincennes appears to have concentrated on these highly popular wares which helped the factory to survive during its difficult early years. In 1748 the factory presented vases of these artificial bouquets to King Louis XV and Queen Marie Leczinska, and the following year the Dauphine Marie-Josèphe de

7.

Calabre cup with lizard handle

Soft-paste porcelain
*c.*1749-53
Cup: H. 7.7 cm; D. 7.5 cm
Saucer: D. 14 cm
(MNC 26,485)

The landscape decoration, as well as the lizard-shape handles, are painted in purple mono-chrome, with touches of gold on the handle.

Saxe gave a splendid bouquet to her father, the Prince-Elector of Saxony. Each flower, differently coloured, was formed petal by petal, attached with slip (liquid paste) to a stem of *cannetille* (twisted braid).

The Vincennes factory was greatly inspired by the designs of Saxon porcelain, yet it seldom reproduced the *Kakiemon** designs of Chantilly. From 1748-9 purple *camaïeux* (monochrome paintings) appeared on pieces, forming an original design that was exclusive to Vincennes: landscapes, still-lifes and children at play, with touches of gold.

Handles and lid stoppers were cast in relief, taking the form of flowers, plants and even small animals, like the lizard of the so-called *calabre cup* (Plate 7). Shaped pieces imitated

8.

Tureen and dish

Soft-paste porcelain
*c.*1750
Tureen with lid:
H. 25 cm; L. 38.3 cm
Tray: L. 54.7 cm
(MNC 23,414)

The tureen and dish, imitations of silverware pieces, illustrate *rocaille* decoration in opposing curves. The flower bouquets still owe inspiration to those of Meissen. ▲

9.

Candle holder

Soft-paste porcelain
*c.*1753-4
H. 8.1 cm; L. 18.4 cm
Decorated by
Louis-Denis Armand,
known as Armand the Elder
(MNC 17,023)

On back:
Mark and letter-date A
Painter's sign = Louis-Denis
Armand the Elder

Camaïeu colours were also used
for moulded pieces such as the
tulip-shaped candle holder. Pink
roses decorate the rim and bowl.

factory. It was Caillat who greatly expanded the number
of available colours thanks to an all-purpose flux (although
not yet suitable for purples or for gold). In 1748 the
Benedictine monk Hippolyte Le Faure sold Vincennes the
'secret for preparing gold, and that of the mordant and
its application'; thus, after 1749, the Vincennes range
increased to sixty colours.

The *palette cup* (Plate 11) made by Taunay was decorated
with small coloured squares, illustrating samples of all the
colours prepared and utilised by the factory during the
summer of 1748. A second *palette cup* (Plate 11b), made
by the painter Louis Armand the Elder, showed experiments in mixing colours, in various thicknesses and trans-
parencies. This piece was also precisely dated 9 July 1749.

The year 1751 proved a turning point for the Vincennes
factory. The successive arrivals of Jean-Jacques Bachelier,
Jean Hellot and Hendrick van Hulst enabled the factory to
cease modelling itself on Meissen and to develop its own
original style. In addition to the beautiful blue – a *grand feu**
colour, opaque and almost violet, the cloudy transparency

comparable items of silverware (Plate 8), with sweeping
curves of *rocaille* decoration (Plate 9).

As at Meissen, the Vincennes factory developed a range of
coloured grounds, initially yellows (Plate 10) – yellow being
an easy colour to spread because it was naturally greasy –
obtained from an oxidised mixture of tin and antimony,
and in due course sky blue, green and violet.

Orry de Fulvy died in May 1751. Over the previous six
years the range of Vincennes colours had evolved steadily.
He lived to see the emergence of several green grounds –
very difficult to create – as well as violet, which Sèvres
would subsequently abandon; but the celebrated *beau bleu*
('beautiful blue' or 'lapis blue') was not perfected until July
1751 by Jean Hellot.

Several businessmen and painters such as Pierre-Antoine
Taunay and Jean-Mathias Caillat sold enamels to the

10.

Mustard pot

Soft-paste porcelain
Mid-eighteenth century
H. 8.4 cm; L. 9.2 cm
(MNC 25,029)

The monochrome blue
decoration on the gilt
surround reserve stands out
from a yellow ground.
It is signed by the painter
Vieillard, one of the factory's
most famous decorators. ▲

11.

Palette cup

Soft-paste porcelain
29 August 1748
H. 6 cm; D. 8.1 cm
Colours used by Taunay
(MNC 6,638)

Signed: *'Inventaire, Fait ce 29
août 1748 à Vincennes.
Taunay fait'*

11b.

Palette cup

Soft-paste porcelain
9 July 1749
H. 4.5 cm
Colours used by
Louis-Denis Armand,
known as Armand the Elder
(MNC 26,501)

Signed and dated on the back

12.

*Bouillard sugar-bowl
and lid*

Soft-paste porcelain
1755 or 1758
H. 9.6 cm; D. 7.6 cm
(MNC 26,493)

The landscape in *beau bleu*
monochrome, done by the
decorator Antheaume (whose
signature is represented by
the figure of a house), created
a stir which helped to make
Vincennes famous. ▲

13.

Bottle coolers

Soft-paste porcelain
1750-2
H. 19.7 cm; L. 26.9 cm; W. 19.4 cm
Gift of the heirs of Mme Poidatz,
1917
(MNC 16,058$^{1-2}$)

The monochrome purple
decoration shows *chinoiseries*
inspired by prints after François
Boucher, as, for example, *Tea*,
one of the oldest bottle coolers
made at Vincennes.

14.

Jardinière, partitioned vase or partitioned Duplessis vase

Soft-paste porcelain
*c.*1752-3
H. 29.6 cm; L. 16 cm;
W. 17 cm
(MNC 25,029)

The decoration shows three scenes of animals on a terrace, inspired by a print of Simon de Vlieger: *Turkeys*. The edges of the *jardinière* are underlined by a delicate line of *beau bleu*.

of which only appeared after firing of the *glaze** – Hellot himself made the coloured enamels (Plate 12) and ensured their exclusivity to Vincennes.

The Vincennes patterns fell into three or four categories: *chinoiseries** (Plate 13) and children at play, usually painted in monochrome, based on the drawings of François Boucher, as well as landscapes and pastoral scenes; birds (Plate 14), either real or imagined; natural flowers (Plate 15); and decorations in gold of ornaments, flowers and flying birds.

The application of gold was the exclusive right of the royal factory, this privilege being more or less respected during the reign of Louis XV. Vincennes' distinctive gilt decoration of birds in flight (Plate 16) and inset foliage was never equalled by other eighteenth-century factories.

Gilding, in which Vincennes excelled from 1751 to 1752 onwards, required a succession of delicate operations. The powdered gold, thinned with a garlic-based mordant, was applied once: fired at low temperature, it was often absorbed, necessitating the application of a second layer.

Gérin's continuous-heat kiln allowed a second, softer firing to be carried out. When this was successfully completed, the gold was burnished, *ie* rubbed with a hard stone, so as to give it its full sparkle. All the borders around the scrolls were then finely chiselled (Plate 17) in order better to catch the light.

15.

Round bottle

Soft-paste porcelain
1754-5
H. 18 cm
(MNC 26,498)

The decoration of small bouquets accentuates the delicacy of this Chinese-shaped, long-necked bottle.

16.

Water jug and basin

Soft-paste porcelain
1753
Jug: H. 24 cm
Basin: L. 34 cm
(MNC 26,318)

This water jug '*à la romaine*', slightly distorted in shape, has a clouded *lapis bleu* ground. In the reserve two golden birds are in flight, and a rich gilt decoration surrounds these reserves.

17.

'Pompadour' pot-pourri
vase (one of a pair)

Soft-paste porcelain
*c.*1753
H. 43.3 cm
(MNC 24,576[1-2])

The two so-called
'Pompadour' pots-pourris
display delicate gilt decoration against a very rare
violet ground, with softly
glinting roses and leaves.

Sculpture at the Vincennes Factory: 1740-1800

ETWEEN 1740 and 1756 Vincennes objects in porcelain clay were modelled in two ways: either moulded piece by piece and assembled by affixing with slip, or thrown by hand and fired in a special kiln. In fact, a number of shaped pieces were decorated with motifs in relief: sprays of prunus blossom, in imitation of certain pieces from Saint-Cloud, like the king's glass cooler; and borders of fruit, as on the turquoise-blue *service de Louis XV* (Plate 18), more obviously influenced by Meissen.

Complex vases and shaped pieces were moulded. The *panier à jours* (plaited basket) (Plate 19) in white, turquoise and gold, which appears in the stock-list of 1 February 1756, was made in the *biscuit** kiln, indicating that sculpture already played an important role in porcelain production.

The first white or polychrome statuettes in soft-paste porcelain were modelled by Jean-Baptiste Oudry and made by Claude Le Boitteux and Pierre Blondeau. In due course François Boucher became the favourite, if not exclusive, painter attached to the factory, his figurines of children and amorous shepherds proving especially popular.

The fairly complex technique of moulding entailed a number of operations and involved several craftsmen. As a rule, the artist's original model, in terracotta, was broken up into as many parts as were required for reproduction.

The modeller prepared individual moulds for each of these parts, using plaster while it was setting, and a cover to hold all the smaller pieces. He laid out the open moulds containing the parts, inserted the flattened paste or *croûte* into each one and gently pressed it down. As it dried, the paste shrank and became firmer. The modeller then brought the two sides of the mould together, sticking the edges of the paste with slip.

Stripping was a delicate procedure. The paste, not yet fired, was still soft. It was now the task of the *répareur** to attach each part of the object as indicated by the original model. To make sure the seams did not show after firing, he would mould a broad groove at each juncture point and fill these

18.
*Oblong dish of the
Louis XV service*

Soft-paste porcelain
1754-5
L. 39 cm; W. 26.8 cm
(MNC 24,777)

The centre has a flower design.
On the rim is a decoration in
relief of redcurrants. A floral
pattern is also painted in the
reserves. ▲

19.
Plaited basket

Soft-paste porcelain
1756-7
H. 20.5 cm; W. 19 cm
(MNC 25,342)

One of the last objects to come
out of the Vincennes factory's
sculpture workshop before the
move to Sèvres.

with fresh paste of the same density as the dried paste, so
that the join became invisible. The skill of the *répareurs* of
the Vincennes-Sèvres factory in carrying out this delicate
operation was unrivalled. When the reassembly work was
complete, all the fragile parts of the figure had to be supported during the firing. After the final firing the piece was
polished with emery paper so that the decorative elements,
flowers, drapes and the like, were brought out in gracefully
minute detail. The application of a variously thick layer of
white or polychrome enamel glaze inevitably coarsened
this decorative effect, and the procedure was abandoned
for good around 1754-5.

Among the more important glazed pieces was the *Deux
Chinois tenant une corbeille* (*Two Chinese Holding a Basket*)
(Plate 20). Measuring 37 cm high, this piece evidences the
difficulty in firing a large piece with a thin enamel glaze.
The glaze tends to crack but, with the second firing, the
enamel is partially refused.

Jean-Jacques Bachelier and Jean-Claude Duplessis
claimed credit for producing a plain, matt biscuit, hence
unglazed, porcelain. Among the first biscuit statuettes,
La Batteuse de beurre (*The Butter Churner*) (Plate 21), by Fernex
in 1754, was a miniature-sized model of stone carvings
in the dairy of Crécy, which he had made in 1752-3 for
Mme de Pompadour from drawings by François Boucher.

L'Amitié au cœur (*Friendship*) (Plate 3), representing the
Marquise de Pompadour as the goddess of friendship, was
also one of the first biscuit figures from Sèvres by Falconet
in 1755. It was offered graciously by the factory to the
woman who inspired it.

At Vincennes, the sculpture studio was directed by Jean-
Claude (the Elder) Duplessis. The role of sculptors such as
Pierre Blondeau and Jean-Baptiste de Fernex was to create
three-dimensional works, after a painting or drawing, most
often provided by Boucher.

The *Enfants Boucher* (*Boucher Children*) was executed in both
biscuit and glazed versions between 1750 and 1755.

Fresh impetus was given to production at Sèvres following
the nomination of Étienne Falconet as head of the sculpture studio, from 1756 to 1766.

20.

Two Chinese Holding a Basket

Large enamelled soft-paste
porcelain piece
*c.*1749-52
H. 37 cm
(MNC 24,564)

The rich fantasy of the basket's motifs and the poses of the loosely draped figures combine to give a baroque feel to this extraordinary sculpture, which may not be by François Boucher. The young Chinese girl, despite her slit eyes, stems from French paintings of the early eighteenth century, and the model of the Chinaman was to be adopted by Le Prince.

21.

The Butter Churner

Soft-paste biscuit porcelain
Model of 1754
By Fernex
H. 19.5 cm
Gift of Mme Yves Le Duc, 1985
(MNC 25,269)

From a sculpture by Gabriel-Christophe Allegrain, made for the dairy of Crécy for Mme de Pompadour in 1753. Three other stone sculptures were made for this dairy by Vassé, Falconet and Coustou, likewise reproduced in biscuit at Sèvres.

This department assumed ever greater importance as Sèvres became famous for specialising in biscuit figures to decorate all manner of useful and ornamental pieces, including commodes, console tables and centrepieces for dinner services.

During Falconet's early years, favourite themes were still the pastoral scenes of Boucher as well as human figures, as featured in the *Cris de Paris* (*Cries of Paris*), for instance: *Marchand de gimblettes* (*Biscuit Seller*) (Plate 22) and the *Petite Fermière* (*Little Farmgirl*), also known as the sixteen *Enfants Falconet* (*Falconet Children*). These were simpler, less sophisticated than those of Boucher. But the pieces comprising the second series of *Enfants Falconet* (Plate 22b) were very realistic, almost cruelly so: they were made from original terracotta models smaller than the first set. The Musée National de Céramique exhibits a large number of terracotta pieces that served as models for these biscuit figures. The factory, too, still possesses a number of old moulds, and gave permission for new casts to be made at the end of the nineteenth century and the beginning of the twentieth century. Falconet also created very graceful, almost baroque, models, such as *La Nymphe à la grappe* (*Nymph with Grapes*) (Plate 23), known as *Erigone et Bacchus*, and its companion piece *Hebe*. The 1759 terracotta is presently in the museum's collection.

The influence of the theatre and comic opera persisted in the second half of the eighteenth century, when the comedies of Charles-Siméon Favart were staged; one of his plays was the origin of the *Nœud de cravate* (*The Bow Tie*) (Plate 24) which the museum possesses both in terracotta and in biscuit. But Boucher remained the inspiration for amorous couples and picturesque groups such as the *Baiser donné* (*Kiss Given*), *Baiser rendu* (*Kiss Returned*), *Chien qui danse* (*Dancing Dog*) and *Lanterne magique* (*Magic Lantern*).

Before he left for Russia in September 1766, Falconet introduced an elegant, virtually neo-classical style, heralded in 1762 by the *Baigneuse* (*Girl Bathing*) (Plate 25) and culminating in *Pygmalion et Galatée*. But somewhat cold allegorical subjects tended to take precedence; *Mélancolie* (*Melancholy*), however, was done after his departure for the court of Catherine the Great.

Jean-Jacques Bachelier took over temporarily as head

22.
First Series of Falconet Children: The Biscuit Seller or the Trinket Seller

Soft-paste biscuit porcelain
Model by Falconet, 1757
H. 14.8 cm
(MNC 15,596)

Not as graceful as the Boucher children, the figures in this first series of Falconet children nevertheless possess a charming sense of naturalism and ingenuousness.

 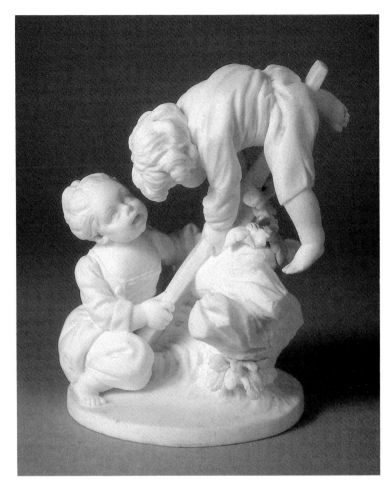

22b.

Second Series of Falconet Children:
The Jacket Game

Soft-paste biscuit porcelain
1760
H. 11 cm
Falconet
(MNC 22,434)

The Swing

Soft-paste biscuit porcelain
1765
H. 15 cm
Falconet
(MNC 17,815)

The second series of Falconet
children depicts the true urchins
of Paris, full of mischief and done
with great realism and comic
verve.

23.

Nymph with Grapes

Terracotta
1759
H. 30 cm
Falconet
(MNC 8,872)

This original terracotta shows the nymph Erigone, seated, three-quarters view, in a very graceful pose.

24.

The Bow Tie

Soft-paste biscuit porcelain
1766
H. 14.2 cm
After Falconet
(MNC 25,227)
and
Original terracotta
1766
H. 14.2 cm
By Falconet
(MNC 7,992)

The title of this group was derived from the play of the same name, by Sainte-Foix. These are the last biscuit pieces from Sèvres to reflect the gallantry and tenderness that eighteenth-century French artists habitually portrayed in their works.

of the sculpture studio, until 1773, while retaining his directorship of the decoration workshop. Louis Boizot and François Le Riche succeeded in turn to the sculpture workshop from 1773 to 1801. In 1775 *Méditation* (*Meditation*) was made, from a model by Boizot, as a pendant to *Mélancolie*. Cast in several sizes, the hard-paste porcelain version of *Méditation* (Plate 26), dated 1785, is now in the museum.

The discovery of hard-paste porcelain, far simpler to manufacture because of its plasticity, enabled the factory gradually to abandon its production of soft-paste statuettes.

The delightful embracing *Vénus et Adonis* (Plate 27) was made by Boizot in 1775. It typifies the talents of this sculptor, showing that he was equally at ease working on either a monumental or small scale.

Portrait busts, too, proved among the more successful products of the Sèvres sculpture workshop. The bust of Louis XV after that of J.-B. Lemoyne (Plate 2), like those of his successive favourites Mme de Pompadour and Mme du Barry, displayed the fine precision characteristic of the Sèvres modellers. Queen Marie-Antoinette was very frequently portrayed, too, both as a young princess and haughty queen.

In 1781, the Marquis d'Angiviller commissioned from Sèvres the series of biscuit statuettes entitled *Hommes illustres* (*Famous Men*), derived from those made in marble for the Louvre Gallery. Most of these original terracottas are today in the Sèvres Museum, including Corneille, Molière, Michel de l'Hôpital, etc. The statuette of Racine (Plate 28), by Louis Boizot, is all the more valuable because the biscuit has never come to light.

Finally, Sèvres modellers satisfied the craving for decorating dinner tables with large biscuit centrepieces in the last third of the eighteenth century: they ranged from the Bacchic centrepieces of Taraval to the grandiose *surtout allégorique du Parnasse* (*Allegorical Centrepiece of Parnassus*) (Plate 29), celebrating the *Apothéose de Catherine II de Russie* (*Apotheosis of Catherine II of Russia*). This joint work by Boizot, Perrotin, Leduc and Mathias, made in 1779, prefigured the ambitious centrepieces of the First Empire.

25.
Girl Bathing

Soft-paste biscuit porcelain
1762
H. 35 cm
Model by Falconet,
1758
(MNC 3,123)

The fashion for biscuit ware at Sèvres in the eighteenth century was in no small measure due to the fact that this type of porcelain resembled marble.

26.

Meditation

Hard-paste biscuit
porcelain
1785
H. (without plinth):
70.5 cm
H. (with plinth):
79 cm
Full-size
From the model by
Louis Boizot in 1775,
made as a pendant to
Melancholy, by Falconet
(MNC 26,362)

Melancholy already
heralded French
neo-classicism,
whereas this sculp-
ture, *Meditation*
(twenty years later),
still retains a some-
what languid charm.

27.

Venus and Adonis

Hard-paste biscuit porcelain
*c.*1775
H. 23.5 cm
Louis Boizot
(MNC 26,309)

Louis Boizot (whose
initials appear on
the hollow of the
plinth) brought a
touch of elegance
and voluptuousness
to his pair of lovers.

28.
Racine

Terracotta
1783
H. 41 cm
Louis Boizot
(MNC 12,975)

Made to the order of the Comte d'Angiviller for the *Famous Men* series, this commission never achieved its expected and merited success. Biscuit versions, colder than terracotta, were in fact in poor demand.

29.

Centrepiece of the Catherine II of Russia service: The Apotheosis of Catherine II, also known as the Parnassus Group

Hard-paste biscuit porcelain
1779
H. 85 cm; L. 68 cm; W. 52 cm
From Boizot
Gift of
Mme Albert Morel
d'Arleux, 1964,
in memory of her son
Pierre Morel d'Arleux
(MNC 23,240)

Boizot had to call on the assistance of Perrotin, Leduc and Mathias to make this centrepiece, a masterpiece of mythological allegory, which crowned the great Catherine II table service.

Sèvres Soft-paste Porcelain Services and Ornamental Pieces from 1756

THE SÈVRES factory, once installed in its new buildings, stepped up its production and introduced a variety of innovations.

Painters and porcelain decorators such as Caton, Antonin Cornaille, Dodin, Vieillard (Plate 30), Denis Levé, Parpette, the Pithou brothers, Capelle, the elder Armand, etc., some of whom had come to Vincennes before 1750, would remain at Sèvres until the end of the eighteenth century.

The most celebrated of the Vincennes-Sèvres wares of this period were the vases. The collection of the Sèvres Museum, though not as comprehensive as that of some museums in Britain, has a good range of them. Although, at the start of the eighteenth century, vases were designed simply as containers for real or artificial porcelain flowers, they later assumed a purely decorative function. The pot-pourri vases, intended to hold sweet-smelling bouquets, were pierced in order to release the perfume of their contents. They were much in vogue under Louis XV, none less so than those called 'Pompadour', like the pair (Plate 17) with a violet ground and sumptuous gilt decoration.

The famous *vase Duplessis* bore the name of the artist and was a model very frequently made at Vincennes. The majority of the Sèvres vases, too, carried proper names: *vase Paris, vase Verdun, vase Falconet,* etc. or names based on their shape: *vase œuf, vase cannelé, vase à colonnes, vase à panneaux, vase ferré* and the like.

Two *vases à panneaux* (panelled vases) (Plate 31) on a blue ground, dated 1767-8, were painted with harbour scenes, very typical of the artist Jean-Louis Morin, in clear, sharp colours. The pair of *vases 'de forme C'* (Plate 32) are ovoid, decorated with two coiled handles. The remarkable *singeries** design is in several tones of gold applied directly on the blue ground, the delicate figures of the monkeys playing in the trees being painted by the elder Armand. The artist, while basing himself upon *chinoiserie* decorations on a black ground in imitation of lacquer, then much in vogue at Sèvres, managed to treat the subject and handle the style in an exceptionally innovative manner.

Popularly known in the nineteenth century as the *vase à*

30.
Palette of the painter Vieillard

Colours used on soft-paste porcelain
Second half of eighteenth century
D. 13.5 cm
(MNC 16,779)

31.

Pair of panelled vases

Soft-paste porcelain
1767
H. (with mount): 38 cm
H. (without mount): 32 cm
(MNC 25,173[1-2])

These harbour scenes in bright, clear colours are among the most successful of Jean-Louis Morin's paintings in this genre. On the back, on a white ground, is a bundle of arms and trophies.

32.

C-shaped vases with singeries decoration

Soft-paste porcelain
1786
H. 29 cm
(No longer with covers)
(MNC 22,461[1-2])

These vases with a *beau bleu* ground are decorated with *singeries* in several tones of gold, by Armand the Elder. Lions and monkeys cavort together in the leafy branches of trees. ▲

l'amour Falconet (*Falconet love vase*) (Plate 33), this vase with a *beau bleu* ground, formed of numerous composite parts, is difficult to date precisely, but was undoubtedly made around 1780. The truncated column with gilded fluting, as well as the sculpted garlands, epitomise the refinement and elaboration of certain Sèvres vases.

Apart from vases, one of the most important areas of production at Sèvres was that of tableware services. Bowls and cups, in particular, were made in large quantities. The *écuelle*, for example, was a covered broth-bowl which came complete with tray. The cup known as a *gobelet* was produced on its own, in various shapes, bearing a proper name, or as part of a *déjeuner* or breakfast set. The *gobelet Bouillard*, for example, was made from the time Vincennes started production.

The standard cup and saucer might be *à la reine* or *calabre*, somewhat flared. The *litron* cup, straight and simple, has been produced from 1753 to the present day.

One type of very small cup was called *mignonette*; this originally applied to a *cup* (Plate 34) decorated by Charles-Nicolas Dodin, in 1764, with its saucer and tray bearing the arms of Aymard de Nicolaÿ and his wife Catherine Lévêque de Graville. The *déjeuners* (breakfast sets) (Plate 35) comprised a milk jug, a sugar bowl, and one or more cups on a tray which, depending on its shape, was entitled *Hébert*, *Courteille*, etc. If it consisted of a large number of cups, the breakfast set might be known as a *cabaret*. The *tasses trembleuses* (Plate 36) from the Delombre collection, fitting into saucers that were hollowed out to hold the cups steady, are variously and richly decorated. The coloured grounds are adorned with polychrome motifs accentuated by gold, *vermiculé** and *œil-de-perdrix** patterns, etc.

Table services eventually brought Sèvres great renown. Vincennes had produced few such services apart from the turquoise blue *service de Louis XV*, begun in 1753, and the first *service de madame de Pompadour*. Shaped pieces included sumptuous oval tureens on stands, round gravy boats, likewise on stands, salt-cellars, mustard pots and covered gravy bowls.

Tableware proper consisted of two sets of plate services: the soup service, with hollow bowls, and the dessert service

33.
Vase with a blue ground, known as the Falconet love vase

Soft-paste porcelain
*c.*1780
H. 43 cm
Salomon de Rothschild
Foundation

Dark blue ground, white and gilt reliefs, polychrome and gilt decoration. The truncated column with gilded fluting exemplifies the neo-classical taste of the period.

34.

*Mignonette cup and saucer,
with a square tray*

Soft-paste porcelain
1764
Saucer: D. 9.5 cm
Cup: H. 5 cm
Tray: L. 11 cm x 11 cm
(MNC 8,853 and 8,854)

The coats-of-arms of Aymard Charles-François de Nicolaÿ were painted, together with those of his wife Catherine Lévêque de Graville, by Dodin. A frieze of egg-shapes linked by stylised palms surrounds the rims of the cup and saucer. A double frieze frames the edge of the square tray.

35.

*Cabaret or Solitaire with scattered
design of roses*

Soft-paste porcelain
1767-72
Attributed to the painter Vieillard
'Calabre' teapot: H. 11 cm
1772
Sugar-bowl: H. 9 cm
1767
'Calabre' cup: H. 6.8 cm; D. 6.8 cm
1767
Saucer: D. 14 cm
Tray with handles: L. 32.8 cm
1767
(MNC 25,627[1-4])

Virtual still-lifes, made up of gardening implements and plants, are painted in the centre of the individual pieces. A scattered design of roses punctuates a *beau bleu* grid which frames all these miniature paintings.

36.

Three tasses trembleuses

Soft-paste porcelain
1763 and 1765
Cup: H. 8.8 cm
Saucer: D. 15.5 cm
Decorated by Micaud
Gift of M. André Delombre,
1955
(MNC 22,292-23,013-23,014)

The decorative variety of these objects conveys some idea of the richness of this lovely collection of *tasses trembleuses: points de Hongrie, passementeries,* gilt braiding and stippling, and roses.

37.

Ice-buckets

Soft-paste porcelain
1787
H. 21 cm
D. 20 cm
Decorated and signed by
Le Guay the Younger,
and gilded by Henri Prévost
(MNC 23,281[1-2])

Made up of three pieces: a cylindrical bucket on three feet, with straight handles; an inner cylindrical dish with rounded rim, resting on the bucket; and a circular cover with a recess serving as the ice receptacle.

with large flat plates. The plates themselves were of metal, like plates for the meat course, for soft-paste porcelain tended to scratch too easily. Ice-buckets with flat lids were fitted with an inner lining of porcelain or metal (Plate 37). They were decorated and mounted in gold. Fruit dishes were of various shapes, square, round or shell-shaped. Other dessert pieces included sugar basins on stands, groups of two or three jam pots and small ice-cream cups. Finally, pails for holding bottles or half-bottles paved the way for a varied assortment of elaborate coolers, culminating in *verrières* or grooved glass-coolers.

The services designed for Madame du Barry in 1770 and for the Prince de Rohan in 1772 were among the most famous, both for the originality of their decoration and for the number of constituent pieces. The *service de Madame du Barry* (Plate 38) consisted of 322 pieces, today distributed among different collections. It was made between 1770 and the end of August 1771. Although the shapes retain the grace of *rocaille*, the antique-style motifs, like the small pale blue *cassolettes*, add a genuinely decorative effect to the double monogram of flowers and gilt.

The great *service de l'impératrice Catherine II de Russie* (Plate 39) was one of the most impressive. Notable for its revival of antique-style decoration, this service was made between

38.

Madame du Barry service.
Ordinary covered tureen
and tray

Soft-paste porcelain
1771
Tureen: L. 32.7 cm; W. 20.5 cm
Tray: L. 45.6 cm; W. 36.3 cm
Legacy of Mr Forsyth Wicks,
1965
(MNC 23,246)

Soup plate

Soft-paste porcelain
1771
D. 24 cm
Decorated by the painter Le Bel
Legacy of Mr Forsyth Wicks,
1965
(MNC 23,245)

Soup ladle

Soft-paste porcelain
1771
L. 32.5 cm
Legacy of Mr Forsyth Wicks,
1965
(MNC 23,247)

This service consisted of 122 pieces in soft-paste porcelain. The painted decoration was by Lebel and Catrice. The rim design was by Augustin de Saint-Aubin, suggesting that he originated the entire project.

39.

*Plate from the service of
Catherine II of Russia*

Soft-paste porcelain
1778-9
Decorated by F. Barré and
gilded by Le Guay the Elder
(MNC 22,602)

Three ice-cups

1779-80
H. 9 cm; D. 7.2 cm
Gifts of the
Comte Anne-Jules de Noailles
(MNC 22,603^1-2)

This was the most important
and most sumptuous of all the
services manufactured by
Sèvres to date. An album of
drawings, in the Bibliothèque
Nationale, includes preparatory
sketches.

1778 and 1779. Its 744 pieces cost 312,217 *livres*. The last,
very late, payment, in 1792, saved the factory from bank-
ruptcy.

The *service dit de Buffon* (Plate 40), made for the Comte
d'Artois in several stages, between 1779 and 1784, is for
the most part kept today in the Camondo Museum. The
celebrated green and gold partridge-eye ground on the
border, known as *décor Taillandier*, was painted by Le Guay
and Vincent, and comprised cartouches adorned with
birds alternating with monochrome profiles. The bird
decoration on the bowl was painted by Chauveaux from
plates by the naturalist Buffon.

40.

Plate from the Buffon service

Soft-paste porcelain
1783
D. 24 cm
Gift of Léopold Double, 1856
(MNC 5,033)

The turquoise blue and gold partridge-eye ground decoration of the border, known as *Taillandier*, was painted by Le Guay and Vincent. The goose design on both bowl and rim was the work of Chauveaux the Elder, based on plates by Buffon.

41.

Lyre pendulum clock

Soft-paste porcelain
1786
H. 61 cm
(MNC 21,649)

This lyre pendulum
clock in dark blue
porcelain has an
enamelled face by
Coteau.

Soft-paste Porcelain Plaques and Stylistic Developments from 1775

FROM the years at Vincennes, the factory had produced toilet articles: shaving bowls with a notch for the neck, holders for soaps and sponges, and make-up or pomade pots, turned out in their hundreds, used to enhance the appeal of the products sold by the perfumers. Water jugs, complete with stands, were produced in a wide range of ingenious shapes, often decorated with gold motifs.

Any article for toiletry, from bed-pans to spittoons, could be made of porcelain: but complete toilet sets, such as those manufactured for the Comtesse du Nord and Queen Marie-Antoinette were rare.

The success of Sèvres porcelain induced the factory to extend its range to even larger pieces, notably painted plaques, used in cabinet-making from 1760 onwards. This fashion persisted for more than twenty-five years. Certain articles of furniture consisted entirely of porcelain plaques, like the famous Carlin commode for Madame du Barry, after Pater, Lancret and Van Loo (in the Louvre). Porcelain plaques were also prominent in the interior decoration of drawing rooms, given pride of place alongside paintings.

Clocks also featured among the glories of Sèvres; restricted initially to the face, porcelain soon became the sole material for the complete clock, as for the *pendule lyre* (lyre pendulum clock) (Plate 41) by Joseph Coteau.

In 1779 Louis XVI commissioned nine hunting pictures from the factory, based on paintings by Jean-Baptiste Oudry. Ten other pictures in soft-paste porcelain were ordered to adorn various of the king's private rooms. Only three of these have been found, painted by the two Pithou brothers in 1782. They are copies based on the paintings of Amédée Van Loo for Gobelins tapestries, entitled *Usages et Modes du Levant* (*Customs and Fashions of the Levant*).

The Sèvres Museum acquired the plaque belonging to Marie-Antoinette, the *Déjeuner de la sultane* (*The Sultana's Breakfast*) (Plate 42), painted by the younger Pithou in 1783 on soft-paste porcelain. Very similar to the picture by Amédée Van Loo, now in the Chéret Museum at Nice, the Sèvres plaque is notable for its marvellously transparent

42.

The Sultana's Breakfast

Soft-paste porcelain plaque
1783
H. 40.5 cm; L. 48.5 cm
Signed and dated
by the painter
Pithou the Younger
(MNC 23,275)

One of the first paintings on
porcelain done by the Sèvres
factory, from the cartoons for
Gobelins tapestries by Amédée
Van Loo, entitled *Customs and
Fashions of the Levant*.

43.

Ewer and basin

Hard-paste porcelain
*c.*1790
Ewer: H. 21.8 cm
Basin: D. 21.8 cm
(MNC 5,291)

The black ground perfectly imitates lacquer; the *chinoiseries* decoration in yellow gilt and platinum is apparently the work of Le Guay.

colours, bringing to the flesh tints a pearly, translucent sheen.

During the second half of the eighteenth century, the influence of Boucher was still very strong, but the impact of Jean-Jacques Bachelier, director of the painting workshop from 1751 to 1793, was apparent in the floral motifs which now emerged as the factory's favourite decorative subject.

Flowers were reproduced in every possible manner, ranging from delicate posies to elaborate bouquets, suspended by ribbons or arranged in a basket, formed into garlands with sprays and arabesques. Then, as the years passed, they became increasingly naturalistic, as on the *service de Talleyrand* around 1780. At the same time, vases and larger objects were decorated with picturesque scenes known as *Téniès*, derived from subjects treated by the Flemish master, Teniers the Younger, qualifying as miniature paintings in their own right.

Chinoiseries and *singeries* were painted on grounds that simulated lacquer, flake, textiles and precious stones, as, for example, the *aiguière et sa cuvette* (ewer and basin) (Plate 43), in imitation of lacquer, and the two soft-porcelain vases, with a *beau bleu* ground, decorated with monkey motifs, by the elder Armand (Plate 32).

44.

Duplessis banded vase

Hard-paste porcelain
*c.*1780-5
H. 48.5 cm
(MNC 24,786)

The *chinoiseries* decoration, on a continuous white band, separated from the pale green ground, is attributed to Lecot. A broad outline of gold, applied flat, surrounds the figures and motifs.

The Appearance of Hard-paste Porcelain and the Triumph of the Antique: 1772-1800

FROM 1772, Sèvres was capable of producing series of services and objects in hard-paste porcelain. However, it was not until 1790 that the technique for producing coloured grounds was perfected. The marks on the back of hard-paste porcelain wares bore the same monogram of interlaced Ls, but they were painted in red or violet and were surmounted by a crown, as, for example, the lovely red mark appearing below a saucer with a black ground, adorned with *chinoiseries*. ▲ On hard-paste porcelain, both the designs and the colours were sharper, the definition less blurred into the body, whereas on soft-paste porcelain the decoration was softer and more iridescent.

The transition to hard-paste porcelain had a fundamental bearing upon the development of form and style during the last third of the eighteenth century. As in sculpture, porcelain bodies tended to become simpler. *Rocaille* was abandoned in favour of the revived antique, often called *Etruscan*. Vases adopted an oval or amphora shape, with simpler handles, as in the three covered *vases Chinois*, in hard-paste porcelain. Their name was derived from the head of the sphinx or from oriental heads originally done from shoulder level. Those in the museum, on a white ground, were decorated with essential features and gilded trophies on one side, and with polychrome scenes of battle on the other, apparently by Charles-Éloi Asselin. The gilded ornamentation was done by Vincent in 1775.

A *vase à bandeau Duplessis* (Plate 44) was made around 1780-5, on a very simple hard-paste porcelain body, in contrast to those of the *vases Duplessis* from Vincennes. A pattern of *chinoiseries* adorns the frieze; the handles are curved in very tight scrolls.

A pair of amphora-shaped vases (Plate 45), dated between 1780 and 1790, are decorated in the antique style, with a pale green frieze. Graceful figures emerge from arabesques of *Salembier* design. The bronze mounts, attributed to Pierre-Philippe Thomire, and the gilding of Henri Prévost complete the boldly classical style of the work.

Finally, there are two highly original *vases Cordelier à fond lilas* (Plate 46), decorated with hunting scenes in *grisaille*,* by Philippe Castel in 1790. These are genuine paintings which run continuously around the vase. The very elegant

45.

Pair of amphora-shaped vases

Hard-paste porcelain and gilded bronze
*c.*1780-90
H. 21.8 cm
Gilder: Henri Prévost
Gilded bronzes attributed to Thomire
(MNC 25,493[1-2])

The design of the figures
emerging from the arab-
esques seems to have been
done by an engraver. The
polychrome decoration is
of rare delicacy.

46.

Pair of Cordelier vases

Hard-paste porcelain
1790
H. (with plinth): 44.6 cm
D. 45.1 cm
(MNC 26,406[1-2])

The *grisaille* decoration on a lilac ground depicts hare-hunting with the gun, less frequently portrayed than hunting with hounds. The decoration is by Drouet and the gilding by Vincent. Philippe Castel, painter at Sèvres of the hunting scenes of Oudry and Desportes, was also inspired by the engravings of Ridinger.

47.

Two-handled cup and saucer

Hard-paste porcelain
1788
Cup: H. 11 cm; D. 10 cm
Saucer: D. 18.7 cm
Decorated by Fumez,
from drawings by
Jean-Jacques Lagrenée for
the dairy of Rambouillet
(MNC 6,795)

The shapes of these pieces were derived from ancient ceramics in the Vivant-Denon collection.

48.

Two-handled cup and saucer from the birds in a small frieze service, black on a yellow ground

Soft-paste porcelain
End eighteenth century
Cup: H. 7.8 cm; D. 8.3 cm
Saucer: D. 17.5 cm
Gift of M. André Delombre,
1955
(MNC 23,033)

Made during the First Republic. On the back, the inscriptions list the name of the birds: *'Grand naquet des Philippines'*.

handles and the ovate pattern around the neck were done by the painter Drouet and the gilder Vincent.

This evolution of vase shapes and styles paved the way for the porcelain created for the dairy of Rambouillet. In 1787 Thévenin designed the famous Rambouillet dairy, to satisfy Queen Marie-Antoinette's craving for nature, as exemplified in the hamlet of Trianon. The Sèvres Museum possesses two *gobelets et leur soucoupes* (Plate 47) based on cantharus shapes from the Vivant-Denon collection, and a bowl in hard-paste porcelain. They were decorated by Jean-Jacques Lagrenée in 1788.

At the very end of the eighteenth century, the factory began to go in for highly ornate polychrome decoration, on grounds imitating the most opulent materials, ornamented with gold and precious metals. Along with flowers, birds were the most popular decorative subjects, as seen, for example, on the plates of the *service aux oiseaux à petite frise noire sur fond jaune* (Plate 48), dating from the first year of the Republic. The two plates of the *service aux oiseaux à fond écaille* (Plate 49), of 1792, also treat this subject. They testify to the consummate skill of decorators such as François Mirey who were working for Sèvres at this period.

During the Revolution and the Directory, the factory, despite major financial difficulties, produced a number of attractive objects (Plate 50) in the eighteenth-century tradition, adorned with a pattern of republican emblems: cockades, ribbons, bundles of weapons and the like.

49.

Plate from the scale service

Hard-paste porcelain
*c.*1792
D. 24 cm
(MNC 12,829)

The *trompe-l'œil*, which imitates scales, is adorned with three gold friezes, done by François Mirey. The central frieze includes delicate grasses.

50.

Covered cup and saucer

Soft-paste porcelain
1794-5
Cup: H. 13.5 cm
Saucer: D. 17.5 cm
(MNC 17,821)

The bundle of arms decoration was painted in grey-green by G. Noël, in white reserves surrounded by a Parma border and a tricolour galloon.

The Factory and
the Museum under
the Direction of
Alexandre Brongniart

51.

Egyptian inkwell

Hard-paste
porcelain
1802
H. 22 cm; L. 26 cm
(MNC 2,648)

One of the objects
made in bronze
paste by Charnou,
decorated in matt
gold.

52.

Insomnia or
The Searcher
for Fleas

Hard-paste
biscuit porcelain,
blue and white
1809
L. 27 cm
Model by Boizot
(MNC 17,829)

The Empire-style
bed and footstool
are blue, accentu-
ating the young
woman's state
of disarray. A
pendant of this
sculpture was
entitled *La Toilette*.

The First Empire: 1800-1815

ALEXANDRE BRONGNIART, son of the architect Théodore Brongniart, who built the Palais de la Bourse, was appointed director of the Sèvres factory on 25 floréal, year VIII (or 14 May 1800), by Lucien Bonaparte, then Minister of the Interior.

Brongniart concentrated mainly on developing the role of the ceramics and glass museum. By 1822, the new museum housed 4000 pieces, administered by the first curator, Désiré Riocreux, a former painter at the factory. Assisted by three chemists, Brongniart published in 1844 the *Traité des arts céramiques*, and in the following year the catalogue of the collections of the Ceramics Museum in 1845. He also initiated exchanges with other factories, particularly between Sèvres and Meissen.

In 1804, Brongniart abandoned for good the production of soft-paste porcelain, pronouncing it too expensive and insufficiently plastic, concentrating on the improvement of the hard-paste body. The quality of the glaze was transformed by the addition of *pegmatite** which, in vitrifying at a very high temperature, took on even greater strength.

Brongniart encouraged the manufacture of other bodies: *pâte bronze* (bronze paste) (Plate 51), developed by Chanou in 1802, which proved short-lived, *dentelle en porcelain* (porcelain lace) and *pâte bleutée* (bluish paste), this last being inspired by the creations of the Wedgwood factory, used, for example, by Boizot in *L'Insomnie* (*Insomnia*) or *La Chercheuse de puces* (*The Searcher for Fleas*) (Plate 52).

In 1819 Brongniart perfected the *coulage** process whereby a more fluid paste was used to manufacture large porcelain plaques.

Changes and improvements to the porcelain bodies led to the introduction of a new palette, including two new ground colours, chrome green, produced in Paris by Vauquelin, and pale blue or *bleu agate* (agate blue) (Plate 53). The increased range of colours after 1820 made it possible to achieve results comparable to painting on canvas, including the faithful transfer of copies of Vatican frescoes onto porcelain plaques.

Gold, too, was used plentifully in decoration. Some cups

53.

Agate blue vase

Hard-paste porcelain
*c.*1810
H. 20 cm
Department of
Art Objects at
the Louvre Museum
(MNC 15,504)

The gold of the stylised flowers, bunches of grapes and decorative motifs is accentuated by the marbled blue ground.

54.

Jasmine cup

Hard-paste porcelain
1812
Cup: H. 9 cm; D. 10.5 cm
Saucer: D. 16 cm
(MNC 1,803)

The portrait of the Empress Marie-Louise was painted after Isabey by Delafosse. The artist managed to convey the fresh allure of the young woman, adorned with jewellery, enlivened by the beautiful gold decoration.

were covered with gold inside, and the rims of plates and saucers were adorned with impressed gilt motifs. This method of impression was introduced by Legros d'Anizy around the beginning of the century. Under the First Empire, Sèvres decorators imitated hard stone, gilt bronze, goldsmith's work in gold and marble and, of course, painting.

Alongside the chemical research and the technical improvements, Brongniart set about creating new, purer and more streamlined shapes. The principal models were the so-called *étrusques* (Etruscan) vases of the Vivant-Denon collection deposited at Sèvres in 1785. Such forms acquired names that became famous: *vase fuseau, vase étrusque carafe, vase étrusque à rouleaux*, etc.

The shapes of cups, too, were modified to good effect. Notable examples were the wide-mouthed, very high-handled *tasse jasmin* (jasmine cup) (Plate 54), on a simple or fluted base, and another cup on a raised base.

During this period the imperial factory attracted a variety of artists, talented decorators who were employed for the genres that suited them best. Thus Nicolas-Antoine-Florentin Le Bel devoted himself to landscapes, Jacobber and François-Pascal Philippine painted flowers, Marie-Victoire Jaquotot specialised in portraits, while Georget, Swebach, Isabey, Constantin and Béranger handled Napoleonic epic subjects.

Vases remained the most representative wares among the many exceptional productions of the Sèvres factory during the First Empire. Particularly noteworthy were the tapered vases created in 1800 by Théodore Brongniart to accommodate, on the belly, a portrait or an important historic scene. Thus the Queen of Westphalia, Catherine of Württemberg, dressed in court costume, was painted in medallion form on a *vase fuseau* (tapered vase) (Plate 55) by Georget in 1812. As a companion piece, another tapered vase, also by Georget (Plate 55b), bore the portrait of the Countess Saint-Jean d'Angély as a Muse playing the lyre. In a wholly different spirit, both the nankeen ground and the pattern of flowers and gilt motifs illustrate the creative imagination of this painter.

The *vase étrusque à rouleaux* (Etruscan scrolled vase) (Plate 56),

55.

*Tapered chrome green vase
with the portrait of
Catherine of Württemberg,
Queen of Westphalia*

Hard-paste porcelain
1812
H. 52 cm
(MNC 1,802)

Georget's painting of
Catherine of Württemberg
in court dress, against a
background of green
drapes and within a gold
frame, is remarkably effect-
ive. Four sphinxes arising
from arabesques appear to
be carved in gold.

55b.

*Tapered vase showing the
Comtesse Saint-Jean
d'Angély as a muse*

Hard-paste porcelain
*c.*1809
H. 54.4 cm (including
plinth: H. 2.5 cm)
(MNC 26,310)

The painter Georget
used the oval space of
the vase to depict the
half-clothed, undraped
Comtesse Saint-Jean
d'Angély holding a lyre.

one of the masterpieces of the Sèvres Museum, perfectly epitomises the contemporary experiments with shapes and new forms of decoration. The shape designed by Percier in 1808 was executed full size, *ie* 120 cm high, in 1813. The belly of the vase is adorned with a large polychrome painting by Valois in the form of a frieze, representing *L'Entrée à Paris des œuvres destinées au musée Napoléon* (*Entry into Paris of Works Destined for the Napoleonic Museum*), such treasures coming from museums in Rome. The famous antique statues of *Laocoön*, the *Medici Venus* and the like, in white marble, are shown being borne on chariots flanked by soldiers of the First Empire in gaudy uniforms. The decorative painter Béranger adorned the neck of the vase with a frieze, comprising ten medallions of celebrated ancient personages, painted as cameos. The handles terminate in scrolls decorated with four medallions in relief representing Augustus, Napoleon, Lorenzo de' Medici and Pericles. In Brongniart's opinion, this vase was 'the most beautiful to have come out of the factory's workshops' and he saved it from destruction in 1815.

56.

Etruscan scrolled vase

Hard-paste porcelain
1813
H. (with handles): 120 cm
Modelled by Percier
Decorated by Béranger
(MNC 1,823)

This famous vase, glorifying Napoleon and his future Museum of the Fine Arts, never left the factory. Undoubtedly destined for one of the imperial residences, the Louvre or the Tuileries, it escaped destruction thanks to the vision of Alexandre Brongniart.

57.

Plate from the Olympian service

Hard-paste porcelain
1805
D. 24 cm
(MNC 1,790)

The central painting is
'Apollo and Daphne' by
Le Guay. The Pompeiian
red rim is adorned with
rosettes alternating with
laurels in burnished gold,
in imitation of antique
designs.

58.

Plate from the Egyptian service

Hard-paste porcelain
1811
D. 23.7 cm
Decorated by Swebach
Malmaison Museum
(MM 2,888)

Ruins of one of the temples
on Elephantine Island in
Upper Egypt are depicted
in sepia monochrome.
The decoration on the rim
features the double crown
of Upper and Lower Egypt,
alternating with a profile of
a bird-god in gold on a blue
ground.

59.

*Plate from the Emperor's
service*

Hard-paste porcelain
1810
D. 24 cm
(MNC 6,528)

The episode depicting the
passage of the isthmus of
Suez by General Cafarelli
(who risked drowning) is
dwarfed by the landscape of
water, the distant buildings
and the vast sky. The
burnished gilt frieze,
comprising swords, laurels
and stars, was designed by
Théodore Brongniart;
applied on the chrome green
ground, it symbolised the
Empire. The 172-piece main
course and dessert service
was made for the exclusive
use of the emperor in three
years (1807-10).

60.

Plate from the gold-rimmed service

Hard-paste porcelain
1813
D. 24 cm
Signed and dated Van Os, 1813
(MNC 2,023)

The natural-sized fruits were painted by Van Os. The frieze of palmettes on the rim in burnished gilt amply justifies the name given to the service. In fact, there were no shaped pieces, only plates made over a period of five or six years.

61.

Emperor's service with different views; Plate showing the palace of the King of Bavaria in Munich

Hard-paste porcelain
1812-13
D. 23.6 cm
Painted by Le Bel
(MNC 6,584)

The rich design of sphinxes and gilt scrolls on the blue rim frames the central painting of the palace façade, marvellously done in oblique perspective. The service contained an unlimited number of plates and was continued under Louis XVIII.

Talleyrand was lavish with diplomatic gifts. Thus two of the most beautiful Sèvres table services were presented to Tsar Alexander I: the *service olympique* (*Olympic service*) in 1807 and the *service égyptien* (*Egyptian service*) in 1808. The Olympic service, apart from a few pieces, is today in the Armouries Museum in Moscow. But the Sèvres Museum possesses several plates that conjure up the appearance of the whole service. The rim is painted in Pompeiian red, highlighted by rosettes and golden laurels. The bowl, left white, is adorned with mythological subjects, recreated from Renaissance frescoes. *Apollo* pursues and embraces a weeping *Daphne* (Plate 57), her arms already terminating in branches. On another plate, the resting Heracles is based on an antique statue.

The *service égyptien* (*Egyptian service*) (Plate 58) was based on drawings made by Vivant-Denon, during the Egyptian campaign. The frieze is conceived as a frame, giving emphasis to the picture shown on the bowl. On the rim, imaginary hieroglyphs and gilt motifs stand out sharply from the blue ground. In the centre, all the subjects are treated in monochrome sepia: they depict monuments of ancient Egypt, including the sphinx and temples, or scenes of contemporary Egypt dating from the Napoleonic campaign of 1798-9.

The most sumptuous of the services made by Sèvres for all the imperial residences is the *service de l'empereur* (*Emperor's service*) of 1810 (Plate 59). The rim is decorated with a famous pattern: a frieze of swords in matt gold on a chrome green ground, a new colour and one of the glories of the imperial factory. This service, the Emperor's favourite, was taken to St Helena. The museum possesses two of its plates.

62.

Plate from the Greek iconographic service, Venus de Médicis

Hard-paste porcelain
1813
D. 23.8 cm
(MNC 1,809)

The profile of Venus, on a lapis blue ground, was painted by J.-M. Degault, in imitation of the famous antique marble bust.

63.

Breakfast set of the Famous Women of Antiquity:
Cup with portrait of Pauline
Cup with portrait of Cornelia
Cups: H. 9.5 cm; D. 8.8 cm
Saucers: D. 16 cm

Teapot with portraits of Berenice and Arsinoë
H. 15.6 cm
Cream jug with portrait of Cleopatra
H. 11.2 cm
Sugar-bowl with portraits of Sappho and Aspasia
H. 12.4 cm

Hard-paste porcelain, 1813-15
Painted by Degault after Visconti
(MNC 23,583)

Composed of seven pieces and a tray, this *déjeuner* decorated by Degault is a masterpiece of its kind. The profiles in monochrome onyx are very delicately rendered against the beautiful clouded lapis blue ground. The tray shows the silhouettes of Penelope at her weaving loom, with her women, lit from behind.

Cup and saucer from the Régnier or Castiglione breakfast set

Hard-paste porcelain
1813
Saucer: D. 15.4 cm
Cup: H. 10 cm; D. *c.*8.6 cm
(MNC 6,160)

Decoration in white biscuit relief on a gold ground. Cup lining in gold. Régnier created a masterpiece with his interplay of biscuit and gold, the design mounted on enamel and biscuit (presented by Emperor Napoleon III in 1864 to the duchesse de Castiglione). ▲

Other services, with prestigious names, such as the *service à marli d'or* (*gold-rimmed service*) (Plate 60) which was executed in stages over a period of several years from 1806 to 1813, and the *service à vues diverses dit de l'empereur* (*Emperor's service with different views*) (Plate 61), dated 1812-13, likewise celebrate epic Napoleonic events, as the paintings, for the most part, represent the towns and provinces of the First Empire.

The *service iconographique grec* (*Greek iconographic service*) of 1813 (Plate 62) has links with ancient Greece and Rome:

Napoleon wished himself represented as the new Augustus. Decorated by Degault, it features cameo profiles standing out in relief from a dazzling blue ground. Compared with these dinner services, the breakfast sets at first glance appear more modest. Yet these pieces, too, in shape and decoration, are splendidly typical of the period.

The *déjeuner* of the *Femmes célèbres de l'Antiquité* (*Famous Women of Antiquity*) (Plate 63) was decorated by Degault between 1813 and 1815. The beauty of the ornamental pieces, coffee-pot, sugar-bowl and milk jug, and the slender

65.

Bust of Napoleon I

Hard-paste biscuit porcelain
1805
By Chaudet
H. 25 cm
(MNC 19,978)

An ideal material for imitating marble, biscuit was admirably suited for showing the emperor, looking austere and impressive, as Augustus or Alexander.

elegance of the cups, serve as a model that was to be developed over the following thirty years. The cloudy lapis blue ground and the gilt and platinum friezes set off to perfection the onyx cameos, reproducing the profiles of Berenice, Sappho, etc. The tray representing *Pénélope surprise par les prétendants* (*Penelope Surprised by the Suitors*) was also painted by Degault after Flaxman.

Another *déjeuner*, done in the same period by Régnier, offers for the first time in the history of Sèvres an extraordinary work in biscuit relief on matt gold. This *déjeuner Régnier* (Plate 64), named after its maker, proved an immediate success. The mark of the imperial factory is here depicted by the eagle and the inscription in red *Mr Imp^{le} de Sèvres*. ▲

The period was not especially noteworthy for sculpture. Under the Consulate, certain illustrious figures were represented in bust form, such as the generals Desaix and Kléber, in 1801, after Boizot. The Emperor himself had his portrait done on numerous medallions, and the museum has a very plain example of his *bust* (Plate 65), in biscuit, after Chaudet. Other versions of this bust, larger and more ornate, also exist. The busts of Josephine and Marie-Louise were made, after Chaudet and Bosio respectively. Of more importance are the biscuit centrepieces of dinner services like that of the *service olympique*, after Taunay, or of the *service égyptien*, representing ancient temples. Unfortunately, the Sèvres Museum only possesses incomplete elements of these. Two biscuit sculptures depicting *Homer and Tasso* (Plate 66), after Callamar, were imperial commissions of 1808, made by Brachard and Oger in 1812. These neo-classical works are in a sense a follow-up to the *série des grands hommes de la France* (*Great Men of France*) of 1783-7, indicating that Napoleon, too, desired to be remembered as an enlightened monarch.

66.
Tasso

Hard-paste biscuit porcelain
1809-12
H. 43.2 cm; L. 32 cm; W. 20.3 cm
By Oger after Callamar
(MNC 26,369)

This sculpture
of the Italian
poet was a
pendant to
that of Homer.

67.

Glass plaque: Sappho playing the lyre

Painted glass
1809
H. 49.5 cm; W: 38.8 cm
Signed and dated:
'E.C. Le Guay P.¹ 1809 Manuf.ʳᵉ Impériale de Sèvres.'
(MNC 851)

One of the first glass-
painted plaques done
at Sèvres.

The Restoration and the July Monarchy: 1815-1848

AFTER the collapse of the First Empire and the exile of Napoleon to St Helena, the Sèvres factory retained a comparatively important role, thanks to the competence of the same director, Alexandre Brongniart, who was astute enough to save from destruction, in 1815, particular works testifying to former imperial splendour.

Between 1815 and 1848 the factory became noted for its great virtuosity. New techniques were introduced; Brongniart, who since 1802 had been interested in *peinture sur verre* (painting on glass) (Plate 67) opened a special glassmaking workshop in 1824. Run successively by Pierre and then Louis Robert, this workshop operated until 1852. A fluted pot with red lustre represents the first attempt at a lustrous glaze by Pierre Robert in 1822.

In the field of porcelain, there were many and varied exceptional pieces, and porcelain plaques were still being turned out in large sizes. These plaques were mounted onto articles of furniture, and so provided extraordinary adornment. Vases, too, were significantly more successful than in the previous period. The Sèvres Museum contains some forty porcelain plaques made between 1817 and 1840. One of the largest plaques, entitled *Bouquet pyramidal et corbeille de fruits* (*Pyramid-shaped bouquet and basket of fruit*) (Plate 68), was executed after a painting by Van Spaendonck. Determined to remain scrupulously faithful both to frescoes and original paintings, Brongniart sent Constantin to visit Rome, in order to copy the frescoes of Raphael and his school at the Vatican. *L'École d'Athènes* (*The School of Athens*) (Plate 69) and *La Délivrance de saint Pierre* (*The Deliverance of St Peter*) were reproduced on plaques 100 cm across.

Constantin also copied the works of French painters such as *L'Entrée d'Henri IV à Paris* (*The Entry of Henri IV into Paris*), after Claude-Charles Gérard, in 1827. All genres, religious and secular alike, could be represented in porcelain: *Psyché et l'Amour* (*Psyche and Eros*) (Plate 70) by Gérard, the original of which was already very smooth and 'porcelain-like', was reproduced perfectly by Victoire Jacquotot in 1824. Still-lifes of flowers and fruits were likewise faithfully copied, like the above-mentioned *Bouquet pyramidal* done by Jacobber

68.

Pyramid-shaped bouquet and basket of fruit

Hard-paste porcelain plaque
1837
H. 110 cm; W. 90 cm
(without frame)
By Moïse Jaccober
after Van Spaendonck
(MNC 7,250)

The original painting by
Van Spaendonck had
been done for Louis XVI.
Housed at the French
Embassy in Berlin, it was
unfortunately destroyed
between 1940 and 1945.

69.

The School of Athens

Hard-paste porcelain plaque
1833
H. 64 cm; L. 91 cm
(without frame)
By Constantin after Raphael
(MNC 7,645)

Painted in reduced size on a
porcelain plaque, the frescoes
of the Stanze in the Vatican
Palace have been faithfully
reproduced; the smooth, shiny
material of the porcelain gives
it renewed freshness.

in 1837 from a painting by Van Spaendonck on a plaque 110 cm high.

Porcelain plaques were also employed in furniture for pedestal tables, writing cabinets, chests and clocks. Two *guéridons* (pedestal tables) dating from 1821 are in the museum. One of them, designed by Jean-Charles Leloy, has geometrical motifs in variously coloured imitation marble. On the second (Plate 71), Jean-Charles Develly painted the erection of the new statue of Henri IV on the Pont-Neuf. Around the central picture, twelve medallions relate the wise words and actions of 'Good King Henri with the white plume'. The artist brought an almost journalistic dimension to the scenes painted in *grisaille* on this circular table, which was designed for the education of the young Duke of Bordeaux.

Ten years later, Develly's colleague Leloy painted a highly refined polychrome decoration for the *coffret du duc de Bordeaux enfant* (*casket of the infant Duke of Bordeaux*) (Plate 72). Of small dimensions, four of the plaques are designed in the style of medallions illustrating the moral virtues, accompanied by explanatory maxims. The central portrait of the boy duke, painted by Régnier, after Béranger, shows the heir to the throne, standing, poised and graceful, in a landscape full of historic evocation.

In 1827 the factory set another landmark with the production of a writing cabinet made entirely of porcelain. Three examples of this piece of furniture were manufactured. The one in the museum belonged at one time to the Bey of Tunis, after having been in the collection of the Duke of Montpensier (one of the sons of Louis-Philippe). Described as a *cabinet ou bibliothèque de lecture pour une femme* (Lady's cabinet or reading stand), it was better known as the *Secrétaire des muses* (*Cabinet of the Muses*) (Plate 73). The main panel, which slides, represents the *Muses on Parnassus*, by Le Guay. The side panels, like the columned and pilastered feet, are in porcelain, supported by metallic frames. The cameo-medallions are likewise in porcelain, executed by Barbin and Durosey.

During the Restoration, vases continued to be spectacularly successful; the pair of *vases théricléens* (*Thericlean vases*) (Plate 74) entailed the use of a new technique introduced by Boudon de Saint-Amand. Crystal medallions, each

70.

Psyche and Eros

Hard-paste porcelain plaque
1824
H. 58 cm; L. 40 cm
(without frame)
By Marie-Victoire Jaquotot
after Gérard
(MNC 7,259)

Brongniart believed fervently that painting on porcelain should not differ essentially from painting on any other surface.

71.

Henri IV pedestal table

Hard-paste porcelain,
gilded, patinated bronze,
wood, velvet
1821
H. 81.3 cm; D. 65.7 cm
Gift of
Albert François-Poncet,
1973
(MNC 23,441)

The porcelain pedestal table is
a model created by Brongniart
in 1821. The central subject is
the erection on the Pont-Neuf
of the statue of Henri IV,
painted by Jean-Charles
Develly. Twelve medallions
around the central painting
illustrate the achievements of
'Good King Henri'.

72.

Plaques for the casket illustrating the education of the Duke of Bordeaux

Hard-paste porcelain
1831
H. 28.5 cm
(MNC 15,664)

The portrait of the Duke of Bordeaux was painted by F. Régnier, after Béranger, on the central plaque surrounded by four other plaques depicting the sciences that the heir to the throne was expected to master.

73.

Lady's cabinet or reading stand (The Muses)

Hard-paste porcelain, gilded bronze
1825-7
H. 190 cm; L. 120 cm
(MNC 23,408)

This beautifully crafted *secrétaire* consists of porcelain plaques supported by bronze frames. The main flap slides open by means of a hidden mechanism. Le Guay painted the picture of *The Muses on Mount Pindus*. Barbin and Durosey painted the ornaments, columns, locks, etc. on porcelain.

containing porcelain cameo-medallions, were mounted onto vases by Jean-Charles Leloy and Pierre-Noël Blaquière, dating from 1818-20.

The *coupe des cinq sens* (*Bowl of the Five Senses*) (Plate 75) is one of the most extraordinary creations of Sèvres. Because of its large size, an illustration can hardly do it justice. This Grecian-style bowl was created in 1806 by Théodore Brongniart, and its iconographic decoration takes the form of a broad circular frieze, designed by Évariste Fragonard and painted in 1825 by Mme Ducluzeau.

Between 1827 and 1832, Béranger painted *L'Éducation physique des anciens Grecs* (*Physical Education of the Ancient Greeks*) on the second *vase étrusque à rouleaux* (Plate 76), as a companion piece to the vase of 1813. This vase, magnificent though it is, was received coldly by one critic: 'Enough of the antique, you have been repeating this for ten years!' At the ensuing exhibition, in 1835, a *vase dans le style de la Renaissance* (*Renaissance-style vase*) (Plate 77) was presented by Évariste Fragonard. Juxtaposing white biscuit and matt gold, the painter created groups of neo-Renaissance cupids and female figures, in generously curved high relief, to produce an astonishing baroque effect.

Sèvres continued to produce large numbers of clocks with increasingly elaborate and detailed decoration. The *pendule d'Anaximandre* (*Anaximander's clock*) (Plate 78), based on a type introduced by Brongniart, in the form of a milestone, has a painted decoration with an historical context. The details of the foliate scrolls above the face, dial, and on the side panels are very delicate imitations of cameos.

The Sèvres factory also produced some delightfully decorated small objects. The hexagonal teapot, known as the *théière chinoise Fragonard* (*Fragonard Chinese teapot*) (Plate 79), exemplifies the inventive humour of Alexandre-Évariste Fragonard, who originated the form. The painter Pierre Huard exploited the colour range by dividing the piece into eighteen faces, with Chinese figures in the centre, and dragon scales or rounded tiles on the lid.

As for tableware, dinner services were supplied for various royal residences, commissioned by the so-called Service du Gobelet (Cup Office). Single cups in the 'jasmine' style retained the popularity they had acquired under Napoleon

74.

Pair of Thericlean vases (named after the Athenian potter Thericles)

Hard-paste porcelain, crystal, gilded silver, gilded bronze
1820
H. 57.5 cm
(MNC 25,247[1-2])

Five medallions representing the most famous French kings, grouped around Henri IV, are inlaid on one of the vases. On the other, five inlaid medallions illustrate princes and princesses of the family of Louis XVIII surrounding this king.

75.

Bowl of the Five Senses

Hard-paste porcelain
1825
D. 95 cm; H. 55 cm (plus base)
(MNC 8,157)

Évariste Fragonard designed the miniature paintings evoking the Five Senses in a Neo-Renaissance setting: the paintings were done by Mme Ducluzeau in 1825.

76.

*Etruscan scrolled vase
('Physical Education of
the Ancient Greeks')*

Hard-paste porcelain,
gilded bronze
1827-32
H. 100 cm; D. 65 cm
(MNC 7,535)

The austerely beautiful
shape of this vase is based
on that of the Etruscan
vase of 1813 (see Plate
56). The scenes painted
on the frieze are divided
by pilasters bearing
antique vases.

77.

Renaissance-style vase

Hard-paste porcelain,
gilded bronze
1834-5
H. 91.5 cm; L. 46.5 cm
(MNC 24,963)

The vase was made by Évariste
Fragonard at the request of the
director, Alexandre Brongniart,
to symbolise the renovation of
the Sèvres factory. Fragonard
produced a piece in which gold
and white were spectacularly
contrasted, the whole sculptured
in high relief.

78.
Anaximander's clock

Hard-paste porcelain,
gilded bronze
1838
H. 75 cm; L. 36 cm
(MNC 16,397)

Alexandre Brongniart had created a type of clock shaped like a milestone, like this one, composed of porcelain plaques mounted inside the bronze, by Béranger. The clockmaker Robin made the face.

ANAXIMANDRE
MONTRE À ANAXIMÈNE
LA MANIÈRE D'ÉTABLIR UN GNOMON

79.

Fragonard Chinese teapot

Hard-paste porcelain
1827
Coloured grounds
Polychrome and
gilt decoration
H. 13.5 cm; L. 17.3 cm
(MNC 24,784)

Between 1806 and 1839 Évariste
Fragonard designed shapes and
decorative schemes for the Sèvres
factory. In 1819 he made the
models of two highly colourful
and baroque 'Chinese' teapots,
which he gave to Pierre Huard
to paint.

80.

A.B. cup and saucer, 1813

Hard-paste porcelain
1816
Cup: H. 9.3 cm
(without handle)
D. 9.5 cm
Saucer: D. 16 cm
(MNC 7,215)

This shape was undoubtedly due to Brachard, more rounded than the 'jasmine' shape which widened at the neck. The purple ground and the gilded decoration were particularly apposite for the medallion portrait of King Louis XVIII.

81.

Breakfast set, variously called 'Anacreontic' or 'Brachard', after the designer of the shapes of the pieces, created in 1812
(Detail on opposite page)

Hard-paste porcelain
1813
Coffee jug: H. 16 cm
(MNC 7,548¹⁻⁸)

The painter Le Guay arranged medallions in imitation of ancient cameos on shapes created in 1812. They show the great Greek and Latin authors (such as Anacreon and Ovid) on a violet ground adorned with arabesques of fruit and foliage in rich polychrome.

82.

Duguesclin breakfast set

Hard-paste porcelain
1835
Tray: L. 45 cm
Teapot: H. 14 cm
(MNC 7,547)

The markedly neo-classical shapes
were by Évariste Fragonard; Leloy
designed, and Barbin painted, the
decorative motifs. Le Guay painted
the tray representing Duguesclin
and his companions-in-arms.

and were often decorated with portraits, which also
adorned heavier pieces, the *A.B. 1813 cups* (Plate 80).

The most original wares produced by Sèvres were still the
breakfast services as, for example, the *déjeuner Brachard ou
Anacréontique* (*Brachard or Anacreontic breakfast set*) (Plate 81)
which revived the shapes and cameo motifs of the *déjeuner
des femmes célèbres de l'Antiquité*. These elegant pieces were designed in 1814 by Brachard, and the splendid polychrome
decoration was painted by Le Guay in 1830. The shapes
adopted for the *déjeuner Duguesclin* (*Duguesclin breakfast set*)
(Plate 82) are flattened and neo-classical, yet the decor-

ation, painted by Leloy, Barbin and Le Guay, is neo-
Gothic, in the 'troubadour' style.

The Sèvres dinner services were sold in large quantities:
for the Château of Fontainebleau alone, there are records
of twenty-eight deliveries of porcelain between 1830 and
1849. Among many original designs was that for the *service
des arts industriels* (*Industrial Arts service*) (Plate 83), painted by
Develly from 1823 to 1835. The plates show various workshops manufacturing porcelain and also the glassworks at
Sèvres. On the museum's two *glacières* (ice-buckets), the
scenes depicting the cultivation and harvest of cacao and

83.

Plate from the Industrial Arts service, showing the workshop of the painters and gilders at the Sèvres factory

Hard-paste porcelain
1823
D. 23.8 cm
Painted by Develly
(MNC 2,872[2])

This decorative scheme is famed both for the splendour of the blue and gold chequerwork on the rim and for its historical context. Other plates show the preparation of the porcelain body, the workshop of the sculptors and mounters, the glass shop (Sèvres bottles) etc.

sugar were both painted by Develly in 1827. The centre of each piece is taken up by a miniature painting, while an intricate blue and gold trellis decoration serves as a frame.

The *service des départements* (*Departments service*) (Plate 84) of 1827, the *service des fleurs* (*Flower service*) of 1828, the *service forestier* (*Forestry service*) (Plate 84b) of 1834 (almost all the pieces of which are in the Topkapi Museum in Istanbul), the *service des productions de la nature* (*Natural Products service*) and the *service des pêches* (*Fisheries service*) (Plate 84c) of 1840 all testify to the abundance of the factory's commissions: these were designed both for the royal court and as dip-

lomatic gifts, destined particularly for the countries of the Near and Middle East.

The fruit bowl from the *service des petits chasses* (*Hunting Small Game service*) (Plate 85) of 1821 shows an original design with a frieze of wild animals in the undergrowth, the details of the different golden colours giving it a sumptuous decorative effect.

On the death of Alexandre Brongniart, the collections of the museum contained some 12,000 pieces.

84.

Plate from the Departments service;
'La Lozère: view from around Mende'

Hard-paste porcelain
1827
D. 23.8 cm
Decorated by A. Poupart
(MNC 13,208)

The rim, with its garlands and medallions on a nankeen yellow ground, is highly original. This dessert service, featuring the national departments, must have comprised a hundred or so flat plates.

84b.

Plate from the Forestry service.
'Egyptian forest of palm trees,
sycamores and cassias';
'View of the Matharé obelisk at the
period of the Nile floods'

Hard-paste porcelain
1834
(Dessert service dating from 1834-41)
D. 24 cm
Decorated by A. Poupart
(MNC 6,591)

Under the Restoration, Sèvres services no longer exalted the sovereign but were seen as genuine miniature paintings.

84c.

Plate from Fisheries service:
'Sardine fishing'

Hard-paste porcelain
1840
D. 24 cm
Decorated by Garneray
(MNC 7,608)

This painter specialised in marine views.

85.
Fruit dish from Hunting
Small Game service

Hard-paste porcelain
1821
H. 22.2 cm; D. 32.5 cm
Painted by Leloy
(MNC 25,235)

The highly original frieze
features sections of undergrowth
in gold, red and brown, cut
hedge-shaped as in a park, each
showing a different wild animal.

Discoveries and Changes at Sèvres during the Second Half of the Nineteenth Century

86.

Elephant teapot

Hard-paste porcelain
1862
By Louis Solon
(MNC 26,508)

Zoomorphic shape in celadon
coloured paste. *Pâte sur pâte*
decoration. Another animal-
shaped teapot is in the Victoria
and Albert Museum.

The Second Empire and the Beginning of the Third Republic: 1852-1876

THE DOWNFALL of the July Monarchy during the Revolution of 1848 occurred almost exactly one year after the death of Alexandre Brongniart in 1847. He had trained his successor, Jacques-Joseph Ebelmen, but the latter died in 1852. Victor Régnault duly took over the factory under the Second Empire, then resigned in 1871. The painter Louis Robert succeeded him until 1879.

The main innovation at this time was that of *pâte sur pâte** decoration, otherwise known as *pâte d'application*. Diluted white porcelain paste or slip was applied in very delicate layers, superimposed on a coloured ground. The slip could itself be coloured with metallic oxides and the decoration finished by carving prior to glazing and firing, to give it further refinement.

Pâte sur pâte was enormously popular in France; it made possible some of the most beautiful achievements of the factory under the Second Empire. Marc-Louis Solon created lovely decorations and amusing shapes, such as the *théière éléphant* (*Elephant teapot*) (Plate 86), which had a willow-green ground and highlights in white paste. In due course he left Paris for England, where *pâte sur pâte* was much appreciated, and established a school there. Taxile Doat, the youngest of the decorators after Gobert and Solon, also produced graceful *pâte sur pâte* figures, like the *Sainte Cécile entourée d'anges* (*St Cecilia surrounded by angels*) (Plate 87).

Coal gradually replaced wood for firing the porcelain bodies. The *coulage* process continued to be used for large pieces and also for making a very fine porcelain body known as *coquille d'œuf* (eggshell) (Plate 88).

Under the Second Empire, the role of the artistic directors broadened its scope. The decorator Jules Diéterle (1840-55) and his successor, the architect Joseph Nicolle (1856-71), revived the shapes of vases inspired by the Italian Renaissance, such as the *vase Bijou* (Plate 89) of 1869, decorated with cameo medallions by Gély, and the *coupe Henri II*, of 1841, in imitation of the style of Saint-Porchaire. They drew on eighteenth-century forms with the *vases Boizot* (Plate 90), adorned with *pâte sur pâte* figures, and they also created totally original forms, like the *vase buire Nicolle* (*Nicolle ewer*) (Plate 91) of 1867. The last vases influenced

87.

Round 'E' plate decorated with
St Cecilia surrounded by angels

Hard-paste porcelain
1880
Decorated by Taxile Doat
(MNC 8,961)

Pâte sur pâte decoration.
St Cecilia, in transparent
veils, plays the organ while
little angels carrying a large
streamer flutter around her.

88.

Zarph reticulated coffee-cup

Hard-paste porcelain
1861
H. 13 cm
Shape designed by
H. Régnier in 1850
(MNC 7,592⁴)

Very thin (eggshell) body,
reticulated, produced by
the *coulage* method.

89.

Bijou vase

Hard-paste porcelain
1862
H. 18.5 cm
Celadon ground,
decorated by Gély in 1862
(MNC 5,964²)

Medallions imitating
cameos, in *pâte sur pâte*.
The shape is that of a
hard-stone Renaissance
vase.

90.

Boizot vase

Hard-paste porcelain
1868
H. 37 cm
(MNC 26,653)

The decorator Solon painted the figure of a nymph rowing a boat, in *pâte sur pâte* on a lilac-pink ground.

by those of the Vivant-Denon collection were the *vases dits campaniformes* (bell-shaped vases) (Plate 92) of 1850, the decoration of which was left matt, fired on biscuit. A pronounced taste for arabesques in the Pompeiian style appeared from 1845 to 1855, in response to the commissions of Prince Jérôme Bonaparte.

The glass-painting workshop was run by Pierre and then Louis Robert from 1824 to 1852. A number of stained-glass windows were produced: for Notre-Dame de Lorette in Paris in 1828, then for the royal chapels of Dreux in 1832 and Amboise in 1843. There was also a workshop at Sèvres, from 1852 to 1872, for fine faïence and for the manufacture of varnished clays.

From 1848 to 1873, a workshop for metal enamelling was directed by Jacob Meyer-Heine, who made the *coupe de Galatée*, from the fresco by Raphael at the Farnesina. His assistant, Alfred Gobert, decorated *three ewers* (Plate 93) in the *Diéterle* form, with blue and pink grounds, and silver mounts. The copper plaque of each piece was covered in plain white on which the enameller painted the eventual enamels in vitrifiable colours.

91.
Nicolle ewer

Hard-paste porcelain
1867 shape
H. 31 cm
(MNC 6,747)

Celadon ground and *pâte sur pâte* decoration by Briffaut and Derichweiler. The handle is composed of two acrobatic female figures.

92.
Bell-shaped vase
(one of a pair)

Hard-paste porcelain
1850
H. 24.5 cm
National Museum of the
Château of Fontainebleau

One of the last vases inspired by those of the Vivant-Denon collection. The coiled handles were by Diéterle; the mat decoration, fired on biscuit, by Favre. The warrior profile shows Greek neo-classical influence, as in the Naples Etruscan vase created by Labrouste.

93.

Three ewers

Enamel on copper
H. 60 cm
Shapes designed by
Jules Diéterle in 1848
(MNC 7,678; 7,506; 7,716)

Alfred Gobert decorated the extremely rare pink-ground ewer in 1873 and the two black-ground ewers in 1873 and 1878.

94.

*Female-figure flower-holder
or lamp-holder*

Hard-paste porcelain
1862
H. 105 cm
Signed: E. Forgeot
(MNC 25,271)

Touches of gold on a celadon
ground. Forgeot re-invented
decorative polychrome
sculptures in which celadon
green predominated.

95.

Plate from Napoleon III service

Hard-paste porcelain
1852
D. 25 cm
Decorated by F. Mérigot
Gift of Henry Monnier in 1923
(MNC 16,780)

The monogram surmounted
by an eagle, framed by
foliage, painted wholly in
gold, is an exceptional piece
of decoration.

There was little portrait sculpture under the Second Empire
and in the early years of the Third Republic. Few biscuit
porcelain portraits were made of the monarchs and their
families, except for the *Prince Imperial*, based on Carpeaux's
portrait. There were, nevertheless, numerous examples of
decorative polychrome sculpture. The *Vénus*, after Pigalle,
was made by Forgeot in graduated coloured slip with white

highlights. Forgeot also fashioned the graceful *figures féminines porte-bouquet* (female-figure flower-holder) or *porte-lumière* (lamp-holder) (Plate 94) as elements of a centrepiece, in 1862. In hard-paste celadon ground porcelain, they were very decorative and broke with the tradition of biscuit statuettes. Other female figures by the same maker were created in polychrome porcelain for other purposes.

Sèvres continued to turn out flatware and ornamental objects for dinner services destined for the imperial palaces of the Tuileries, Compiègne and Fontainebleau, a notable example being the *service de l'empereur* (*Napoleon III service*) (Plate 95), decorated by F. Mérigot in 1852 and, in 1854, the *service des petits vues de France* (*Pocket Views of France service*).

96.
*Main building
(Ceramics Palace)
of the new factory*

97.
*Covered passage from
the new factory to
the workshops*

Removal of the Factory and the Museum to their Present Buildings and the Discoveries of Vogt and Lauth: 1876-1897

URING the early years of the Third Republic, the Sèvres factory and its museum embarked upon a new era. In 1876 both establishments moved into new buildings on the banks of the Seine. Félix-Alexandre Laudin, the government architect, had been commissioned in 1861 to erect a prestigious building for the reception of visitors and accommodation of collections, as well as workshops and laboratories, at the foot of the Parc de Saint-Cloud. More than fifteen years later, the Ceramics Palace (Plate 96) was finally opened. The sober nature of the architecture, somewhat surprising for the time, was doubtless dictated by financial considerations. The interior, however, was spacious and stately, epitomised by the great central salon on the first floor from which visitors were conducted smoothly through a succession of public rooms. Direct access from the ground floor of the museum to the factory workshops was provided by a covered passage (Plate 97), rather like a glasshouse, which has now disappeared.

From 1880 onwards, Carrier-Belleuse, a sculptor by training, created a series of large objects in a simple style that provided ample scope for decoration. Other pieces dating from the 1870s looked back to the earlier years.

The pair of *vases de Rhodes* (Plate 98), decorated in 1874 by Barriat with draped or seated figures and branches of pink flowers on a white ground, is a fine example of the traditional Sèvres style.

The two tall *vases Bertin* (Plate 99), made before 1878, reflected the harmonious style of 1850; one was decorated by Gély with a sumptuous bouquet in *pâte sur pâte* which stands out strongly against the black ground; the second was decorated, likewise in *pâte sur pâte*, with a peacock, its tail spread out magnificently on the celadon ground. In addition, two small elephants' heads were added in the guise of handles.

The *vase commémoratif de la nouvelle manufacture* (*Commemorative vase of the new factory*) (Plate 100) also bore a beautiful design in *pâte sur pâte*, white on a deep pink ground. Although the allegorical figures are very graceful, it is hard to repress a smile at the *putti* intended to represent the factory workers.

98.

Rhodes vase
(one of a pair)

Hard-paste porcelain
H. 95 cm
Painted by
Barriat in 1874
(MNC 18,246²)

Against a white ground, allegorical figures hold branches of pink flowers touched with gold. Neck and foot are decorated with blue flowers on a turquoise green ground.

99.

Bertin vase

Hard-paste porcelain
1876
H. 111 cm
(MNC 7,702)

Gély's *pâte sur pâte* decoration on a black ground gives the monochrome roses a silky, naturalistic effect.

The inscriptions on the vase read: ...OIRE DE L'ANNÉE 1896 (left), INAUGURATION DE LA NOUVELLE M... (right), and MANUFACTURE NATIONALE DE SÈVRES.

100.

*Commemorative vase
of the new factory*

Hard-paste porcelain
1876
H. 96 cm
Decoration by Larue
(MNC 9,265)

Pâte sur pâte, rosy-white ground.
Gilt inscription. This vase was
made on the inauguration of
the new buildings in 1876.

101.

Pompeiian vase: 'Day'

Hard-paste porcelain
1884
H. 32 cm
Shape by A. Carrier-Belleuse, 1882
Pâte sur pâte decoration by Auguste Rodin
(MNC 8,522)

Due to the extreme
subtlety of Rodin's
style, this vase is less
obviously decorative
than those made
by the factory's
customary artists.

102.
Kin-te-tchin decorated vase

'Lauth-Vogt'
porcelain
1884
H. 35.5 cm
(MNC 9,232)

Square *flammé* vase, mounted in bronze gilt. Such vases were extremely popular towards the end of the nineteenth century.

103.
'B' violet vase

'Lauth-Vogt' porcelain
1883
H. 19 cm
Flammé decoration, bronze mounting
(MNC 9,247)

Copper-red *flammé* decoration, fired by reduction or by oxidisation, discovered at Sèvres in 1845, was a notoriously difficult and 'secret' process.

Ornamentation of the simple shapes created after 1880 by A. Carrier-Belleuse, like the *vase Saigon* or *vase Pompéi*, was strikingly varied. The most famous of the *Pompeiian vases* (Plate 101) was the one decorated by the sculptor Auguste Rodin who worked at Sèvres from 1879 to 1882 and again in 1888. The *pâte sur pâte* design was incised to give the illusion of space and depth.

In 1880 the chemist Georges Vogt, assisted by Charles Lauth, inaugurated a major innovation. They developed a body capable of being fired at a lower temperature, *ie* 1280°C, suitable for *demi-grand feu* enamels, which fused better with the glaze than on the body which Brongniart had to fire at 1400°C. The *pâte Lauth-Vogt* or *porcelaine dure nouvelle* contained a strong measure of quartz. Vogt pursued his independent experiments with this new body and eventually discovered a formula for *flammé** copper-red glaze. *Flammé* pieces (Plates 102, 103) based on either oriental or western forms were to become very fashionable from 1883 to 1893 and met with great acclaim at the *Exhibition of Decorative Arts* in 1884.

105.

Plate from the Lobé service

New hard-paste porcelain
1888
D. 25.5 cm
(MNC 9,148)

On a body created in 1886, Bonnuit painted a rich floral decoration designed by Habert-Dys.

104.

Crystalline decoration (detail of a bowl from the Sandier period)
(MNC 15,815)

Crystalline decoration was fashionable throughout Europe around 1900.

At the same time, another discovery, due originally to a fault in firing, came to be used as decoration: *crystalline** glazes (Plate 104), appearing from contact with zinc oxide, became a speciality of Sèvres during the last fifteen years of the century. Non-figurative *flammé* and crystalline styles were signposts to the future, which for the time being would preclude representation of the human form.

Meanwhile commissions for dinner services continued for the Élysée and as diplomatic presents. The material remained unchanged, as in the *service Lobé* (Plate 105), in hard-paste porcelain, with sinuous shapes and patterns centred on vegetable motifs. The vibrant colours, extending over the entire surface, heralded the arrival of Art Nouveau.

106.

Chinese bottle experimental vase

Stoneware
Bottle shape and decoration, 1897
Made by Giordan
(MNC 10,915)

The ground of this research vase was
fired at high temperature and engraved
in a remarkable turquoise overglaze.

Alexandre Sandier: 1897-1916

ALEXANDRE SANDIER was trained as an architect at the École des Beaux-Arts in Paris from 1862 to 1868. After several visits to the United States, he returned for good to Paris where he established himself as a talented interior decorator. At the *Exposition Universelle* of 1889 he submitted a plan for a monumental staircase and began a collaboration in that same year with the Utzschneider faïence factory at Sarreguemines.

In 1897, when Sandier took over the post of director of Works of Art at Sèvres, where he would remain for almost twenty years, his reputation was such that he was virtually given a free hand by successive factory directors to pursue his objectives.

The Universal Exposition of 1900 proved a great success for the factory which submitted objects with four different bodies: *grès** (stoneware), *porcelaine dure ancienne* (old hard-paste porcelain), *porcelaine dure nouvelle* (new hard-paste porcelain) and *porcelaine tendre nouvelle* (new soft-paste porcelain).

The *vase d'essai* or *bouteille chinoise* (*experimental vase* or *Chinese bottle*) (Plate 106), in stoneware, was one of Sandier's first productions. The *flammé* decoration, realised by 'raising' or engraving, took the form of waves and water-lily leaves mingling under an iridescent turquoise glaze. The *grand feu* decorations (Plate 107) on traditional hard-paste porcelain plates were confined to fairly pastel tones. The new porcelain, on the other hand, could be decorated in bright colours, without risk of deformity: they included *flammé* flowers, crystalline designs, touches of *pâte sur pâte*, etc. To reinforce the effect of colour, some objects were made partly of porcelain and partly of stoneware.

The museum collection contains more than 320 pieces made under Alexandre Sandier. From 1896 to 1915 the department turned out more than 300 new designs, either by Sandier himself or, prior to his arrival, by Joseph Chéret and J. Chaplain. Indeed, even while technical research was proceeding on the four above-mentioned ceramic bodies, Sandier was planning entirely new forms. Irrespective of whether the vases were large, exceeding 100 cm in height, like the *vase de Dijon*, or small, like the *vase de Chevilly carré*

107.
Plate (detail)

Hard-paste porcelain
1901
D. 24.4 cm
Decoration painted by É. Grodecœur
(MNC 26,402)

The flowers are very typical of the graphic quality of Art Nouveau.

(Plate 108), the forms were always simple. Decoration was dictated by the contours of the vase and contributed to its overall harmony. Thus the naturalism of the blue lupins around the *Chevilly vase* almost conceal its function. And on the pair of *vases d'Aulnay* (Plate 110), nasturtium leaves and flowers twine upwards and spread out on the expanding neck. A final consideration was that the object should be made in a single session, without any adjustment or correction. Straightforward descriptive names were applied to the shapes of these vases: in addition to those already mentioned, for example, were the *vase d'Igny*, the *vase du Bourget* (Plate 109) and the like.

Artists such as Louis Trager, Henri Lasserre, Louis Mimard, Gébleux and Ulrich painted sinuous vegetable and floral motifs, sometimes adding a few insects, but virtually no human or animal figures appeared on the vases during this time.

Actually, the adoption of the Art Nouveau style by Sèvres was not wholly convincing. The simple, restrained shapes imposed by porcelain did not lend themselves happily to the fantastic, sometimes frenzied, forms of decoration so suited to contemporary works in wood, glass or metal. Only stoneware allowed more freedom and came closer to naturalism, as, for example, the *vase aubergine* (Plate 111), made in 1900 by Louis Kahn, with its crystalline glaze decoration. Hector Guimard chose stoneware for three ornamental works for the factory, including the monumental *jardinière colonne* of 1902 (now in the museum at the factory) and the small *vase de Cerny* (Plate 112) with blue and green crystalline glaze.

108.

Chevilly square vase with plain handles

New hard-paste porcelain
H. 23 cm
Shape by Alexandre Sandier, 1898
Decoration by Maurice Naret,
after Herbès, 1908
(MNC 16,173)

The decoration of blue flowers and monochrome brown and green leaves was painted over the glaze at low temperature. At this period the use of gilt highlights was rare.

109.

'B' Bourget vase

Soft-paste porcelain
1895
H. 18 cm
Shape by Alexandre Sandier, 1898
Decoration by Uhlrich,
after Mlle Rault, 1901
(MNC 16,072)

On a white ground, the pattern of trefoil leaves, in green and pink, entwines itself around the vase. The *petit feu* enamels are highlighted in gilt.

110.

Pair of Aulnay vases

New hard-paste porcelain
H. 20 cm
Shape by Alexandre Sandier,
1897
(MNC 10,847)

The nasturtiums design,
by Henri Lasserre, dates
from 1901. On the neck
the leaves blend with the
pale grey border.

111.

Aubergine vase

Stoneware
1900
L. 19 cm
By Louis Kahn
(MNC 15,809)

The shape of the vase, the
texture of the colours and
the crystallisations convey
an overall *trompe-l'œil*
effect.

112.

Cerny vase

Stoneware
1904
H. 27.5 cm
Shape by H. Guimard
(MNC 15,813)

The crystalline decoration
of blues and greens, on a
yellow ground, splendidly
evokes mother-of-pearl and
the ocean depths.

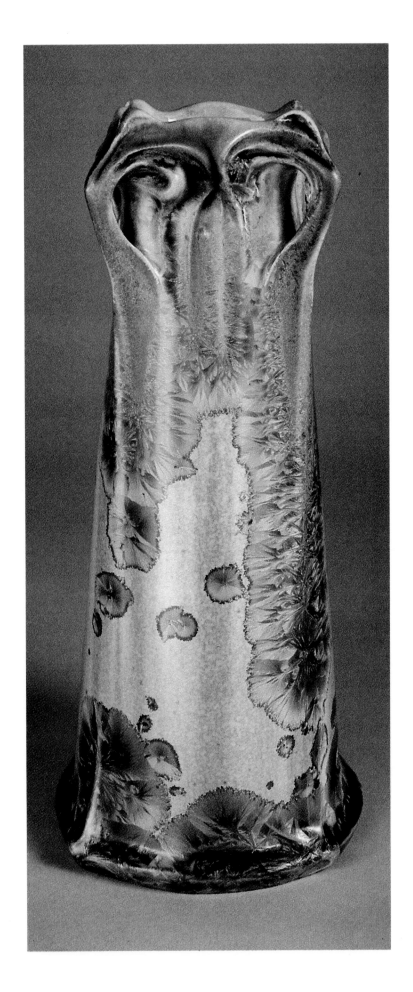

113.

Three dancers from the
Scarf Game centrepiece

New biscuit porcelain
H. 48.3 cm
Full-size
Model by Agathon Léonard, 1900
(MNC 17,260[b]; 16,216; 17,263[b])

Editions of 1905 and
1914. In imitation of
third-century antique
Greek sculpture,
Léonard applied a
soft material which
seems almost moist
and attached to the
bodies of the dancers.

114.

Labourer with upright shovel

Stoneware
H. 18 cm
Model by Dalou, 1903;
1914 edition
(MNC 15,514)

The material captures admirably the realism of the original sculpture.

Sculpture made a comeback in around 1900, during the Émile Baümgart administration, and would develop still further under Émile Bourgeois. The biscuit centrepiece, the *Jeu de l'Écharpe* (*Scarf Game*) (Plate 113) by the bronze sculptor Agathon Léonard for the Exposition of 1900, enjoyed immense success. The fifteen dancers and the swirl of scarves and veils were designed to immortalise the movements of the dancer Loïe Fuller, then all the rage. These dancers were cast in three different sizes and there was a steady demand for their reissue.

In a completely opposing style, the naturalistic sculptures (Plate 114) by Jules Dalou were also executed in reduced size, in ceramic stoneware, from 1903 to 1914.

Finally, from 1895 and during the ensuing years when Alexandre Sandier was transforming the style and production of Sèvres, the forgotten technique of soft-paste porcelain was revived. The enameller Thesmar, who had an independent studio in the factory, decorated soft-paste porcelain pieces with transparent coloured glazes overlaid on gilt foil, or even *cloisonné*. His *vases couverts Saigon* (Plate 115) and small cups adorned with flowers in coloured enamels were particularly original.

115.

Covered Saigon vase

New soft-paste porcelain
1895
H. 24 cm
Enamels in relief by Thesmar
(MNC 10,486)

On the porcelain paste of Sèvres, the enamel fuchsias, dragonflies and grasses appear perfectly balanced.

Sèvres in the

Twentieth Century

International Exhibitions and Porcelain in the Industrial Age: 1920-1964

116.

Tray

Hard-paste porcelain
1920
D. 32 cm
Decoration on a military theme
'2 août 1914 - 28 juin 1919'
Drawn by Lt Jean Droit and
painted by Eugène Lagriffoul
(MNC 18,683)

The simple portrayal of the somewhat ungainly characters and the bright colours bring an air of rural calm to the decoration of this tray.

117.

Rapin night-light

Hard-paste porcelain
1923
H. 43 cm
Shape and decoration by Rapin
Made by J.-B. Gauvenet
(MNC 25,496)

When illuminated, this object is completely transformed; the porcelain colour warms to orange.

THE IMPETUS to Sèvres ceramics production provided by Alexandre Sandier lasted almost until the outbreak of the First World War. The objects made between 1910 and 1920 were, for the most part, simply straightforward repetitions of the modern style, as developed by Sandier.

Direction of the factory, after the death of Émile Baümgart in 1909, was entrusted to Émile Bourgeois, a fervent admirer of eighteenth-century biscuit ware. He revived that style and the museum possesses a large collection of such pieces.

After the International Exhibition of Turin in 1911, however, stoneware was increasingly employed for interior decoration, as, for example, in the boudoir designed by René Lalique.

The First World War completely shattered any opportunity for new ideas since the factory was forced to divert its activities for more than three years towards making stoneware receptacles for acids, components of nitrous explosives. As a memorial to those difficult years, a Sèvres service consisting of a tray (Plate 116) and eight plates in porcelain, entitled *Quelques bons souvenirs des mauvais jours* (*Some Happy Memories of Bad Days*), was issued. It was designed by Lieutenant Jean Droit and painted by Eugène Lagriffoul.

In 1925, at the International Exhibition of Modern Decorative and Industrial Arts, Sèvres exhibited a large selection of works in classic materials. Many of these porcelain objects were novel insofar as they exploited the translucid qualities of the material. Utilised in a luminous fountain, a lampshade, a ceiling light, a bracket-lamp or a standard-lamp, porcelain took on a new lease of life. The *applique de lumière Rapin no. 6* (*Rapin wall-sconce*) of 1921 and the *veilleuse Rapin* (*Rapin night-light*) (Plate 117) of 1923 both stemmed from the collaboration of two artists, Jean-Baptiste Gauvenet and Henri Rapin, and were very typical Art Deco creations.

The series of dancers designed by Jean-Baptiste Gauvenet and decorated by Marcel Prunier likewise resorts to this highly geometrical style. The *Danseuse no. 3* (*Dancer*) (Plate 118), with her short hair, her transparent gold-braided

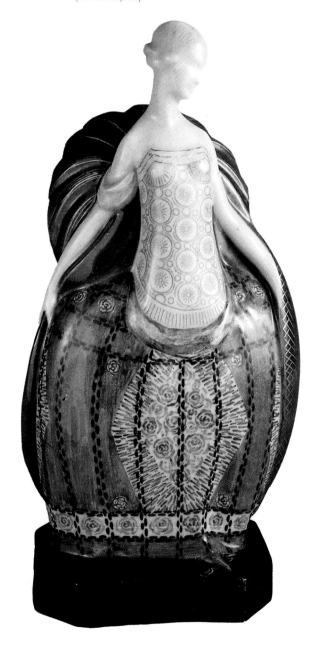

tunic and her voluminous acid-green cape, fully symbolises the happy-go-lucky interwar years.

The forms of biscuit ware particularly reflected the geometrical trend and the influence of the Cubist movement, although somewhat late in the day. Thus the *Dame à l'ombrelle* (*Woman with the Umbrella*), from a model by Charles Maillard in 1925, transformed the somewhat affected original into a charming triangular-shaped object.

The sculpture of the *Joueuses de boules* (*Boule Players*), by de Gaumont in 1920, and that of the *Fruits d'or* (*Golden Fruits*) (Plate 119), by Mlle L. Heuvelmans in 1923, both of them parts of a table centrepiece, are powerfully and poetically evocative.

Enamelled white faïence, a material little employed by the factory, did, however, inspire Cubist sculptors. The famous *Ours* (*Bear*) by François Pompon was made around 1928, in small format, 40 cm in length. Even more geometric, with very evident *craquelure*,* the *Chat* (*Cat*) (Plate 120) was made by the brothers Jan and Joël Martel in 1929.

The vases of the interwar period illustrate strikingly the progressive passage, both in porcelain and stoneware, of a style generously based on curves from the end of the Sandier era to one that was more graphic, *ie* the Art Deco style. The *vase d'Ormesson couvert* (*Ormesson covered vase*) (Plate 121) is perfectly harmonious, with the ovoid curve of the belly, the domed lid and the sinuous lines of the decoration. Louis Gébleux painted the blue peacocks, back to back, between the medallions which extend downwards in narrow lines. The body of the vase is punctuated by soft, feathery plumed decoration, done in *pâte sur pâte* by C. Pilhan in 1921.

Diametrically opposed are the vases of the following decade: the *vase Ruhlmann* (Plate 122), the *coupe Rapin no. 3* (*Rapin cup*) and the *vase Fontaine no. 2* (Plate 123). Whether the vase is bowl-shaped, inverted bell- or cylinder-shaped, the decoration is marked by great simplicity: broken lines suggest water, stylised wavy lines symbolise either a coiffure or the scales of a fish.

Stoneware was utilised by Zoltan Kiss for his rounded relief sculptures: *Don Quichotte et Sancho Pança*, a model of 1936,

119.

Table centrepiece:
The Golden Fruits
(central group)

Hard-paste biscuit porcelain
1923
H. 34 cm
Modelled by L. Heuvelmans
(MNC 17,516)

The influence of the Art Deco style brought greater simplicity to pieces in biscuit porcelain.

120.

Cat

Tin-bearing faïence
1929
H. 33 cm
Modelled in the round
by the Martel brothers
(MNC 25,617)

With this cat, simplicity of structure results in a geometrical shape.

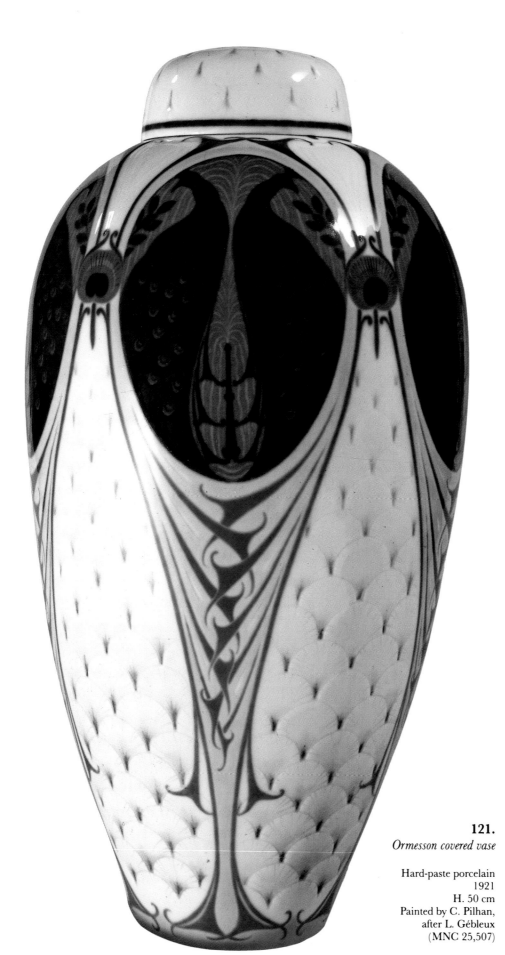

121.

Ormesson covered vase

Hard-paste porcelain
1921
H. 50 cm
Painted by C. Pilhan,
after L. Gébleux
(MNC 25,507)

The velvety surface of the vase, the areas of monochrome blue and the softness of the whites combine to produce the illusion of plumage. For this vase Louis Gébleux created a decorative scheme still influenced by the sinuous 1900 style.

122.
Ruhlmann vase

New hard-paste porcelain
1927
H. 50 cm
Decorated in *pâte sur pâte*
by Anne-Marie Fontaine
(MNC 17,718)

Inspired by the
shape of an
opening flower,
the expanding
lines of this bowl
give it an elegant
appearance.

123.

Fontaine vase no. 2

Hard-paste porcelain
1933
H. 27 cm
Decoration in
monochrome browns by
Mlle Beaudoux, after Goor
(MNC 18,509)

Here the 'African
landscape' decoration,
like the shape, is
somewhat severe.

124.

The Shepherd

Soft red stoneware
H. 23 cm
Group in the round
Model by Zoltan Kiss, 1926
1939 edition
(MNC 17,845)

Zoltan Kiss made
three models of works
in stoneware, bringing
an unexpected touch
of humour to the
principles of Cubism.

and the *Berger* (*The Shepherd*) (Plate 124), done over several years for the factory. Stoneware was also the medium used for bodies of vases, particularly the one created by Maurice Gensoli in 1933, adorned with scrolls and triangles hollowed into the material itself.

In order to prosper, Sèvres, which became an independent enterprise from 1927, had to continue to be innovative and creative, integrating the decoration of its production with contemporary life styles. But table services during the interwar period were arguably less important and less innovative than objects designed for interior decoration. The *service à café* (coffee set) (Plate 125) decorated by Mme Balik in 1925 thus relies on shapes that were established back in 1912: the geometric flower motif is painted in dark shades of green and black.

On the other hand, objects such as *flacons de toilettes* (toilet bottles) (Plate 126), tea caddies and lighting accessories all enjoyed popularity from their Art Deco motifs. Indeed, Sèvres stamped its mark of prestige and distinction on all manner of luxury articles designed for the home.

Jean Mayodon and Maurice Gensoli skilfully adapted ceramics to prevailing architectural tastes. Mayodon, for example, designed a ceramic screen for a small room, and Gensoli decorated a restaurant with porcelain panels from floor to ceiling!

Drawings in watercolours show the intense activity of the Sèvres artists. In the museum, a vase in biscuit porcelain, decorated with athletes, painted in black and matt browns, reveals this particular aspect of Mayodon's talent.

Unfortunately, the great financial crisis of 1929, followed by socio-political problems, virtually paralysed the development of the factory and brought a temporary end to its autonomy in 1941. During the Second World War the factory pursued its everyday activities, compelled to fulfil the commissions of the Vichy government and of particular German generals. The *vases de Lallemand* (Plate 127) in white porcelain were decorated with gilt transfers by Decaris. They illustrate work in the fields and in various crafts, reflecting the moral principles of those years. Sculpture was dominated by the figure of Jean-Baptiste Gauvenet, who brought dynamic movement to the

125.

Coffee set

Hard-paste porcelain
1921-5
Shape of 1912
Decoration by Mme Balik
Coffee-pot: H. 16 cm
Sugar-bowl: H. 10.5 cm
Cream bowl: H. 6 cm
Cup: H. 5.8 cm
Saucer: D. 10 cm
(MNC 17,021)

With its decoration in black, and almost summary floral motifs, this is a classic expression of the Art Deco style.

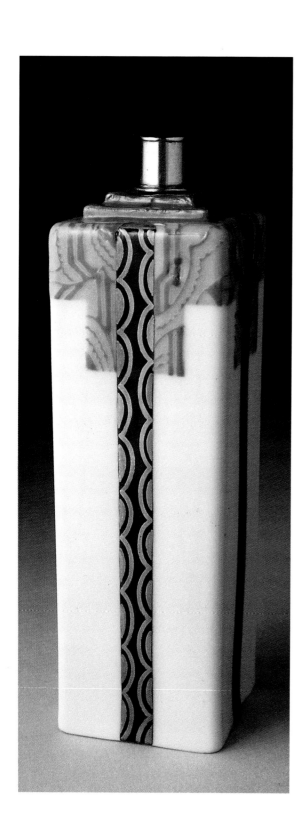

126.

Toilet bottle

New hard-paste porcelain
1925
H. 17.5 cm
Shape and decoration
by Éric Bagge
(MNC 25,540)

The subtle colours add to
the charm of this graceful
object.

127.

Lallemand vase

Hard-paste porcelain
1944
H. 21.5 cm; W. 22.2 cm
(MNC 25,573)

The Craftsman, from a
model by Decaris, im-
pressed in gold on a white
ground. Under German
occupation, the factory of
Sèvres was compelled to
work, as throughout its
history, for those who
wielded power.

128.

Siren

Glazed stoneware
1940-5
H. 24.5 cm
Sculpture in the round
By J.-B. Gauvenet
(MNC 25,580)

One of the factory's artists, Gauvenet turned out reliable work.

129.

Aubert vase no. 2: The Harvest

Hard-paste porcelain
1945-7
H. 30.6 cm
Decorated by Mme Trannoy-Métayer
(MNC 25,609)

This vase represented one of the new shapes created by Émile Decœur.

rounded lines of his glazed stoneware objects, such as the *Sirène* (Plate 128), done between 1940 and 1945.

Émile Decœur created numerous new shapes (Plate 129) which Sèvres was to exploit for more than twenty years. Jean Mayodon, too, designed various forms, not all of which were carried through.

Revived activity in sculpture was further exemplified by the great marine centrepieces of Antoine Orlandini and Henri-Albert Lagriffoul. *Dauphins et Mouettes* (*Dolphins and Seagulls*) (Plate 130) was made in 1950 by Lagriffoul in hard-paste biscuit porcelain, and was made up of three parts: a principal section of *Hippocampes et Naïades* (*Sea Horses and Naiads*), surrounded by two smaller sculptures, *Naïades et Mouettes* (*Naiads and Seagulls*), possibly conceived as a modern response, much reduced in size, to the *bassin de Neptune* (*Basin of Neptune*) at Versailles. The horses, with their passion and power, seem deserving of a more important stage than a dinner centrepiece: a miniature swansong, perhaps, of figurative sculpture.

Sèvres succumbed to the allure of abstract décor between 1950 and 1954. Repeated motifs, like musical fugues, appeared on vases with very simplified lines. Globe shapes like that of the *vase Mayodon no. 31* (Plate 131) or the more rounded form of the *vase Mayodon no. 66* (Plate 132) both proved popular. The *vase bouteille Gensoli no. 7* seems like an

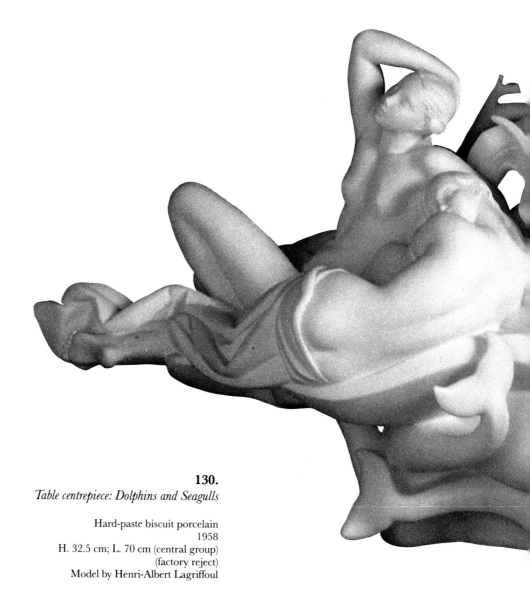

130.
Table centrepiece: Dolphins and Seagulls

Hard-paste biscuit porcelain
1958
H. 32.5 cm; L. 70 cm (central group)
(factory reject)
Model by Henri-Albert Lagriffoul

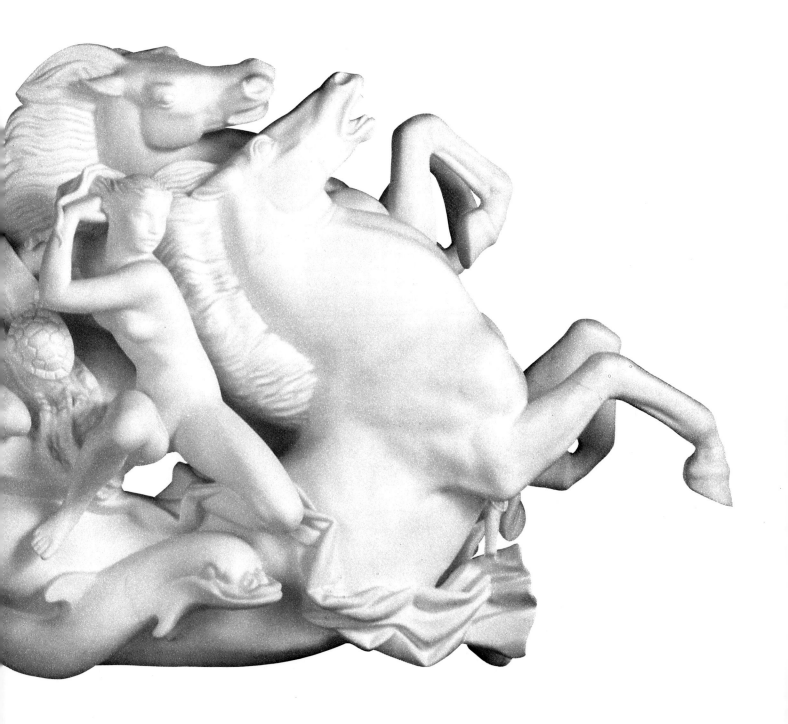

131.
Mayodon vase no. 31

New hard-paste porcelain
1960 shape
H. 42.3 cm
Full-size
Black vermiculate decoration,
drawn with pen, by Claude Boulmé
(MNC 25,484)

132.
Mayodon vase no. 66

Stoneware
1954
H. 40 cm
(factory reject)
From a shape by Mayodon;
decorated by Plantard

inflated version of the latter. The *Gensoli no. 3* and *Gensoli no. 9* forms show a clear demarcation between neck and belly; but the former is generally rectangular whereas the latter is narrow, restricted at the neck as at the base.

Decorators such as Marcel Prunier, André Plantard (Plate 132), Éliane Trannoy-Métayer (Plate 133), Claude Boulmé, etc. were obviously influenced by the pastel-toned designs and sharp graphic qualities of Picard-le-Doux, Carzou, Lurçat and even Léonor Fini. But after 1960,

dominant colours of black and gold on a coloured ground gave way to abstract or geometric lines, narrowly defined or *vermiculé*, on a pale ground: white, beige, yellow or grey. Ornamental objects attracted younger artists like James Guitet and André Beaudin, the latter executing the decoration for the dark blue *vase Decœur* (Plate 134).

At present the museum unfortunately does not possess a complete collection of form examples from this highly interesting period.

133.
Métayer vase no. 3

Hard-paste porcelain
1959
H. 29 cm
(factory reject)
Shape by Métayer;
decorated by Marchal

134.
Decœur vase no. 28

Lapis blue ground
1966-72
H. 38 cm
(MNC 25,361)

Ovoid belly narrowing at the
shoulder; decorated with gilt
triangles, cut by lines of force, in
gold; by Mahiéddine Boutaleb,
from a model by André Beaudin.

135.

Diane dinner plate

Hard-paste porcelain (PAA)
1969-70
D. 26 cm
Petit feu decoration by A. Calder
(MNC 25,369)

Edition limited
to 48 specimens.

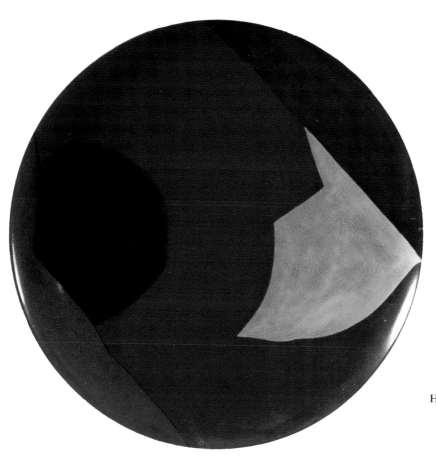

135b.

Diane dinner plate

Hard-paste porcelain (PAA)
1969
D. 26 cm
(MNC 25,459)

Petit feu polychrome
decoration, from
original gouache
by Poliakoff;
edition limited to
48 specimens.

Contemporary Artists and Sèvres in the Second Half of the Twentieth Century

DURING the two decades after the Second World War, the Sèvres factory (under the directorship of Léon-Georges Baudry), concerned to put its affairs on a sound economic footing, became largely self-sufficient, seldom calling on outside decorators. Subsequently, with the appointment of André Malraux as Minister of Cultural Affairs and successively under Serge Gauthier and Jean Mathieu, orders increased and some distinguished artists were invited to Sèvres to create porcelain shapes and designs.

Painters and sculptors such as Zao-Wou-Ki, Agam, Viera da Silva, Serge Poliakoff, Alexandre Calder and Pierre Alechinsky chose, each according to his individual character and talent, different forms of expression. Calder and Poliakoff selected bright colours in the *petit feu** palette for their *plates* (Plates 135, 135b), translating their genius for them into this newly found material. Zao-Wou-Ki and Alechinsky, although employing a large range of colours, exploited the graphic quality that came naturally to them. The rapid and nervous brushstrokes of Georges Mathieu were readily recognisable in the sumptuous gold flourishes that decorated the white *assiette Diane à bord découpé* (*Diane plate with jagged edge*) (Plate 136). Similarly, James Guitet employed very narrow, graduated gold stripes, in the manner of a hatched etching, on a white ground, for his decoration of a *cabaret* or tea service (Plate 137).

Étienne Hajdu alone assumed total responsibility for his objects, designing new shapes, spraying decorative motifs on a blue ground with white reserves, and personally creating the *grand feu* decoration (Plate 138) for the pieces of the *service Élysée* from 1970 to 1976. Hajdu combined metal and porcelain for the *soupière émaillée blanche de Georges Pompidou* (*Georges Pompidou white enamel soup tureen*) (Plate 139), inside a coronet of nickel-plated bronze, with matching lid. He had already devised and used the same principle of metal handles for his vase with green struts on a blue ground.

Equally original, the *cabaret* or coffee set (Plate 140) by Jean Filhos also combined porcelain work with motifs in relief and mounts in embossed silver (which, while being fired, caused the factory's artisans responsible for assembling the components considerable headaches).

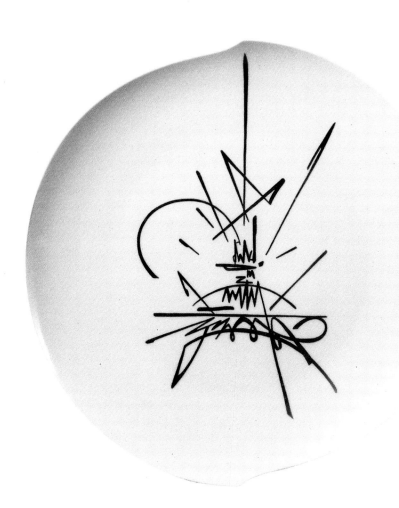

136.

Diane plate with jagged edge

Hard-paste porcelain (PAA)
1967
D. 26 cm
(MNC 25,434)

Gilt decoration applied on white ground; from a model by Georges Mathieu.

137.

Litron tea service

Hard-paste porcelain
1965 shapes
Teapot: H. 13.5 cm
Sugar-bowl: H. 12 cm
Coffee-cup: H. 5.2 cm; D. 5.5 cm
Saucer: D. 11 cm
(MNC 25,402[1-3] or 25,403[1-3])

Gilded decoration by James Guitet, 1970. The hatching and the tight chequered pattern give a modern feel to the decoration.

138.

Diane service

Hard-paste porcelain (PAA)
1970-6
Étienne Hajdu; five decorated pieces; sprayed blue ground around a white reserve
Large bowl: D. 39.7 cm
(MNC 25,420)
Dish: D. 35 cm
(MNC 25,419)
Dinner plate: D. 16 cm
(MNC 25,423)
Dessert plate: D. 22.5 cm
(MNC 25,422)
Salad plate: L. 21.5 cm
(MNC 25,424)

Hajdu created a master-piece, thus far unique, by firing both the body and the decoration at high temperature.

139.

Soup tureen

Hard-paste porcelain (PAA)
1972-3
H. 32 cm; D. 42 cm
Shape and decoration
by Étienne Hajdu
(MNC 25,412)

Prototype made for
President Georges
Pompidou.

140.

*Coffee set with relief motifs
and silver mounts*

Hard-paste porcelain (PAA)
1975
by Jean Filhos
Coffee-pot: H. 18.5 cm
Sugar-bowl: H. 13 cm
Cup: H. 7.8 cm
Saucer: D. 14.5 cm
(MNC 25,378[1-3] and MNC 25,616[1-2])

Jean Filhos combined
his talents of modern
arcanist and silver-
smith to produce this
very delicate and
original coffee set.

141.

Vase no. 4; Dream amphora

Hard-paste porcelain
1966
H. 48.7 cm
(MNC 25,354)

Decoration painted in
polychrome *petit feu*,
predominantly blue,
brown and yellow, by
R. Sivault, from Jean
Arp. Edition limited
to ten specimens.

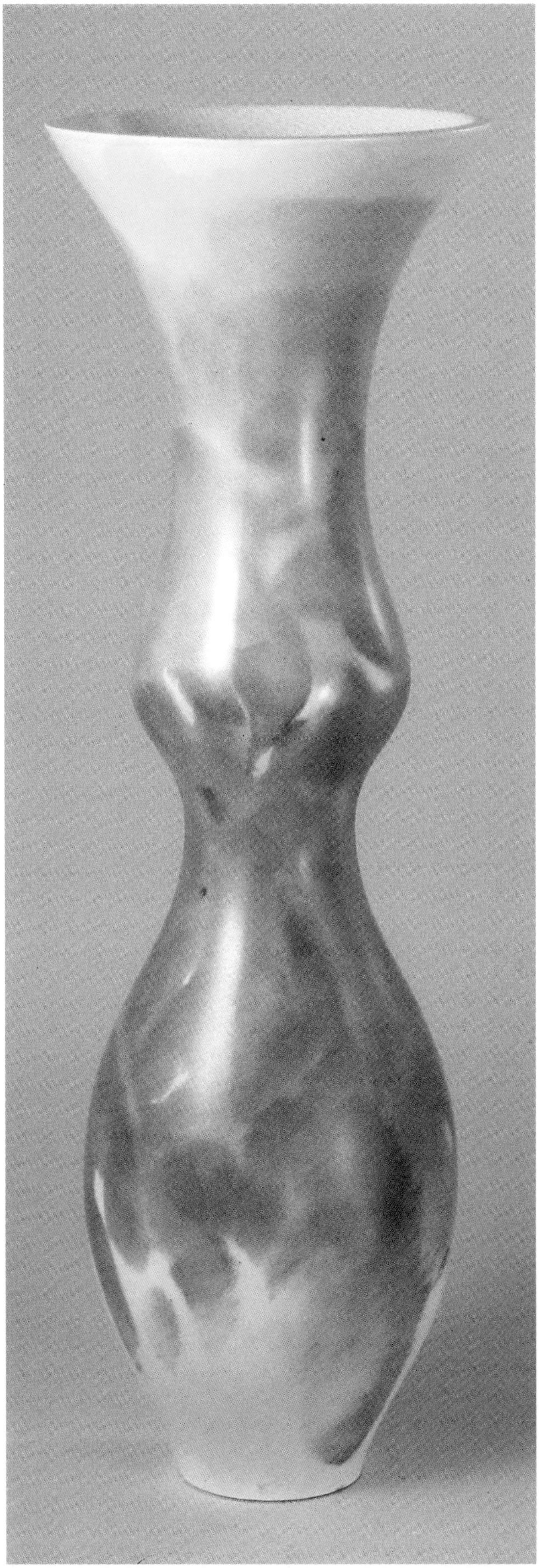

142.

Clock

Hard-paste porcelain (PAA)
Designed by Marc-Antoine Bissière
(Loutre), 1972; made 1973
H. 48.5 cm
(MNC 25,490)

Composed of three
plaques, one for the
face, the other two
for the clowns.

143.

Coffee-pot

Soft-paste porcelain
1982 model
H. 18 cm
(factory reject)

Shape by Adriaen Saxe;
decorated with orange veining
by Gilles Bouttaz, 1991.

More classical and of the same period, the sculptor Jean Arp modulated different volumes on his *vase no. 4 amphore de rêve* (*Dream Amphora*) (Plate 141) and his *Objet casanier no. 2* (*Household Object*), which were reproduced in various materials: in porcelain with *petit feu* decoration, in semi-glazed white porcelain and even in stoneware.

Alongside its table services and vases, Sèvres continued its traditional production of clocks. In 1973, Marc-Antoine Bissière, known as Loutre, made an elegant *clock* (Plate 142) consisting of three enamelled porcelain plaques: the first, in blue, formed the ground and bore the white face; the two others represented the silhouette of two clowns in white costume with large black spots.

Just as amusing as this clock, the series of coffee-pots by Adriaen Saxe was made for ARC, an experimental re-search and manufacturing studio founded by Jack Lang and run in 1982 by Georges Jeanclos. These slender pots with a broad spiralling belly, on a square stand, were painted in warm or acid colours, or even, like the one in the museum (Plate 143), decorated with tiny veins in imitation of hard stone.

Even more than the combinations of metal and porcelain, reused from time to time at Sèvres, the creation of a new,

144.

Rectangular plaque

Hard-paste biscuit porcelain
1970
H. 54 cm; L. 45 cm
Made by Arthur-Luiz Piza
(MNC 25,454)

Bas-relief decoration within a
crescent moon. Edition limited
to ten specimens.

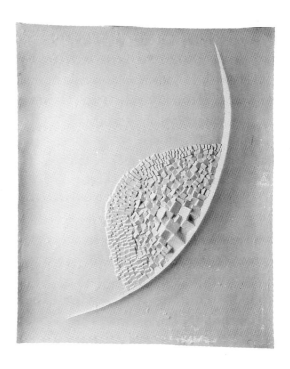

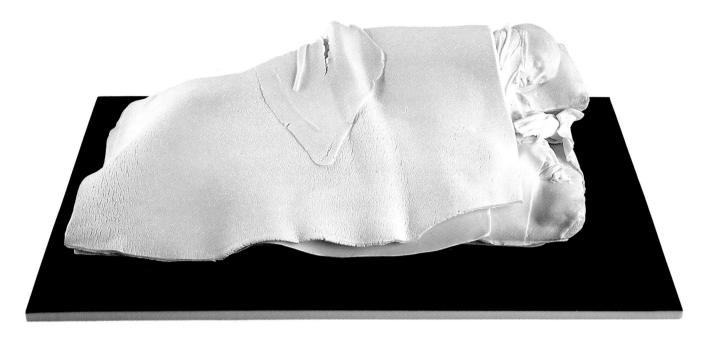

145.

Sleeper

Hard-paste biscuit porcelain (PAA)
1979
On a glazed blue plaque, 1980,
by Georges Jeanclos
Plaque: L. 58.5; W. 43.5 cm
Biscuit: L. 48 cm; W. 33 cm
(MNC 25,430)

This modern recumbent figure aptly symbolises the unalterable nature and infinitely varied guises of porcelain, so rich in promise for the future.

very white porcelain body, known as '*pâte AA*' after the initials of its maker, Antoine d'Albis, enabled the factory to produce some remarkable pieces, both in biscuit and porcelain.

François-Xavier Lalanne produced his astonishing *Autruches-bar (Ostriches Bar)* at Sèvres, in biscuit porcelain and in metal. This zoomorphic domestic bar, in the form of ostriches, opens out to accommodate bottles and glasses. This decorative item of furniture, standing 140 cm high and almost 200 cm wide, was to become world famous. The fine effect of another work by Lalanne, a table centre-piece of *Canard et Nénuphars (Duck and Water-lilies)*, is accentu-ated by the metallic leaves around the porcelain.

Anne and Patrick Poirier drew inspiration from the *surtout égyptien (Egyptian centrepiece)* of 1808 to recreate, in 1978, a large centrepiece entitled *Ruines d'Égypte (Ruins of Egypt)*. They used part of the ancient moulds of the earlier centre-piece to compose seven different adjustable elements: four ponds surrounded by columns, a temple, two pyramids,

two staircases and two colossi, extending for a length of 369 cm. This centrepiece was made in the new hard-paste PAA body.

Arthur-Luis Piza, with his *plaque rectangulaire au croissant de lune (Rectangular plaque within a crescent moon)* (Plate 144), is both painter and sculptor. The plaque, in hard-paste biscuit porcelain, is strangely supple in appearance, like a gently undulating hill. The crescent moon hollows out a deep area of shadow; all the light is concentrated at the top of the plaque and on the assembly of immaterial objects, viewed from above, like a dream.

The *Dormeur (Sleeper)* (Plate 145) by Georges Jeanclos was also done in hard-paste (PAA) biscuit porcelain in 1979, on an enamelled blue *grand feu* plaque made in 1980. This sculpture is a marvellous example of the plasticity of this body, as faithful as an original plaster cast and as bright as marble: each mould was retouched by the artist. Jeanclos directed the experimental research workshop from 1982 to 1988.

The Most Important Marks of Vincennes and Sèvres as Depicted on the Back of Pieces Illustrated in this Book

Vincennes mark in blue; double monogram surmounted by a garland: *c.*1750

Dish: MNC 23,414 (Plate 8)

Vincennes mark in blue; double monogram containing letter 'A': 1753-4

Mustard pot: MNC 25,029 (Plate 10)

Vincennes mark in blue; double monogram containing letter 'B': 1754-5 (the 'royal' year beginning in summer, according to the movements of the Court from Versailles to other residences). W is the mark of the flower painter Vavasseur the Elder, 1753-70.

Oblong dish: MNC 24,778 (Plate 18)

Vincennes mark in blue, without letter date, with signature of the painter Jean-Jacques Antheaume, representing a house.

Sugar-bowl: MNC 26,493 (Plate 12)

Sèvres mark in red; double monogram containing two letter dates ii: 1786-7, and the signature in the crescent of the painter Armand the Elder.

One of the C-shaped vases: MNC 22,461 (Plate 32)

Sèvres mark in red; crowned double monogram, with initials LG of the painter Étienne Charles Le Guay (known 1771-1840).

Hard-paste porcelain saucer: MNC 22,952

Sèvres mark in reddish-brown, under First Empire; crowned imperial eagle with inscription: *Manufacture Impériale Sèvres*, 1813-15.

Régnier or Castiglione breakfast set: MNC 6,160 (Plate 64)

Appendices

Glossary of Technical Terms

ARCANIST: a workman who possesses special knowledge of a secret process of manufacture (as applicable, for example, to porcelain production).

BISCUIT: a once-fired ceramic body, left bare, without glazing.

CHINOISERIE: a European decorative art style, reflecting oriental motifs, akin to the rococo, popular in eighteenth-century Europe.

COULAGE: technical procedure, successfully adopted at Sèvres after 1819, whereby the very liquid ceramic paste, on drying, shrank to such an extent as to allow the ceramic body to be moulded with ease.

CRAQUELURE: the deliberate appearance of small decorative cracks in the paint or enamel of a ceramic object.

CRYSTALLINE GLAZE: form of ceramic decoration obtained by the development of crystals, resulting from mineral salts contained in the glaze.

FLAMMÉ: form of decoration entailing the use of a flame-like copper-red glaze to approximate oriental glazes, developed at Sèvres in the late nineteenth century.

GLAZE: the vitreous coating, constituted of silica and fluxes (such as feldspar), covering ceramic objects, which renders their surface non-porous and provides a decorative effect. The colours in glazes result from metal-oxide pigments which, when fired, are transformed from pale or greyish tones to brilliant hues. Underglaze colours are painted directly onto the biscuit body. Overglaze or enamel colours are painted on top of an already glazed and fired body – both types are then fired to develop the colours and fuse them to the ceramic body. As enamel glazes require lower firing temperatures than that necessary for underglaze, the range of enamel colours is far more extensive. The term enamel glaze is often coupled with *soft-paste porcelain* as the latter fires at a lower temperature than is required for *hard-paste porcelain*.

GRAND FEU: procedure of firing decoration onto porcelain at high temperature (over 1000°C). The colours employed were made with a base of metallic oxides, notably cobalt, which gives blue; manganese, giving black through tones of violet-brown; antimony, giving yellow; copper oxide, giving green; ferrous oxide, producing rust-red; and tin oxide, giving white, principally used for its opacity. Ground colours were often fired *grand feu*.

GRÈS: ceramic stoneware, hard, opaque and resonant, containing a high proportion of silica and clay.

GRISAILLE: painted decoration in monochromatic tones simulating cameos or sculpture. On ceramics, this is achieved by applying layers of varying density white slip or glaze over a dark monochromatic ground.

HARD-PASTE PORCELAIN: porcelain produced by a combination of kaolin, quartz or silica and feldspar. Kaolin is a pure white clay that constitutes the body; quartz or silica is a grease remover and gives the paste its translucence; feldspar acts as a flux.

KAKIEMON: name of a Japanese ceramist whose decorations were much appreciated and imitated in Europe in the first half of the eighteenth century. In France the Chantilly factory successfully reproduced the so-called *Kakiemon* decoration, usually painted in iron red, blue-green, pale blue, violet or greyish-yellow.

KAOLIN: a fine white clay, also known as China clay, which is the essential ingredient of hard-paste porcelain (*pâte dure*).

MARKS: the identification marks used at Vincennes-Sèvres from 1745 to the present day have used a somewhat complex system (Marcelle Brunet's *Les Marques à Sèvres* is the best reference work). During the eighteenth century the double monogram of Louis XV with letter-dates was distinctive, as was the later imperial eagle mark of the First Empire. Subsequent marks were printed in different colours according to the material, sometimes with dates. They generally appeared on or under the glaze, on the back or underside of the object.

ŒIL-DE-PERDRIX: the partridge-eye decoration was peculiar to Sèvres, comprising circles in gilt, punctuated by a central dot, on a white or coloured ground.

PÂTE SUR PÂTE: a decorative technique in which designs are built up in low relief by painting layers of porcelain slip (a liquid paste material called *barbotine*) onto the ceramic body. The slip can be either white or coloured, the latter usually called *pâte colorée*. It was a costly process, demanding the drying of each layer before the application of the next. The composition could be further refined after drying by fine engraving by hand.

PEGMATITE: a variety of feldspar, one of the mineral ingredients of granite. With quartz, it is an essential component of hard-paste porcelain and its glaze.

PETIT FEU: second, low-temperature, firing of decorated piece, subsequent to the firing of the paste and glaze, used for producing a variety of soft colours.

PORCELAIN: a vitrified, non-porous and translucent white ceramic. Porcelain is produced by firing kaolin (white china clay) and a feldspathic stone at a high temperature (from 1250°C) to fuse them together in a glassy mass. The body was then generally covered with a thin glaze and fired before the application of subsequent enamel glazes and/or gilding, which necessitated further firings. The key ingredient, kaolin, was only available at Sèvres from the very early 1800s and permitted the production of a true or hard-paste porcelain.

RÉPAREUR: skilled workman employed at Vincennes-Sèvres factory to attach the various elements of the object after firing, fill in the seams with fresh paste, and finish the object overall.

ROCAILLE: a style of eighteenth-century decoration based on contemporary artificial rockwork and shellwork, the definition later broadened to include the more extravagant aspects of the rococo.

SINGERIE: a decorative style in which monkeys are depicted.

SOFT-PASTE PORCELAIN: low-fired translucent ware produced in Europe from the fifteenth to the eighteenth century, made from a frit and a preparation of opaque clay paste. The piece could then be covered with a transparent glaze and refired. The absence of kaolin in its production distinguishes soft-paste from hard-paste porcelain.

VERMICULÉ: form of ornamentation based on irregular fine or wavy impressed lines, resembling worm tracks.

Directors of the Sèvres Factory from the Nineteenth to the Early Twentieth Century

Alexandre Brongniart (1800-47): mineralogist, devotee of science and the arts. His distinctive policy of stylistic excellence and technical expertise paved the way for the factory's subsequent reputation and commercial success.

Jacques-Joseph Ebelmen (1847-52): technician, successor to Brongniart, who died before making his mark.

Victor Régnault (1852-71): technician, director of the factory throughout the period of the Second Empire.

Louis Robert (1871-9): painter, director of the glass workshop, later provisional director of the factory.

Charles Lauth (1879-87): chemist, inventor of various technical improvements, but unpopular with the workforce.

Théodore Deck (1887-91): renowned ceramist, appointed director on the insistence of the workforce.

Émile Baümgart (1891-1909): capable administrator who defined the objectives which Sandier brought to fruition.

Émile Bourgeois (1909-20): long-time curator of the museum who promoted a policy of producing modern versions of older biscuit wares.

Georges Lechevallier-Chevignard (1920-38): long-time librarian of the museum, under whose direction the factory made extraordinary progress, acquiring legal and financial independence in 1927.

Directors of art projects

Jules-Pierre-Michel Diéterle
chief artist 1840-2
head of art projects 1852-5

Joseph Nicolle
head of art projects 1856-87

They completely renovated the Sèvres style under the Second Empire.

Albert Carrier-Belleuse
director of art projects 1875-87

He created new vase forms.

Joseph Chéret
temporary director of art projects 1886 and 1887

Alfred Gobert
director of art projects 1887-91

Jules Coutan
director of art projects 1891-5

Jules-Clément Chaplain
director of art projects 1895-7

From the artistic point of view, their role was of short duration and of minor importance.

Alexandre Sandier
director of art projects 1897-1916

He introduced the so-called Art Nouveau style to Sèvres in 1900, creating forms and decorations entirely suited to the criteria of the factory's production of vases and occasional pieces.

The National Factory of Sèvres from 1938 to 1992

Directors:

Georges BASTARD (1938-9)

Louis LONGCHAMBON (1939-40)

Guillaume JANNEAU
(administrator of the Mobilier National)
(1940-3)

Max TERRIER (1943-6)

Maurice SAVREUX (1946-7)

Léon-Georges BAUDRY (1948-63)

Serge GAUTHIER (1964-76)

Jean MATHIEU (1976-83)

Robert BIZOT (1983-92)

Curators:

Denis-Désiré RIOCREUX (1823-72)

Jules-François-Félix HUSSON,
known as CHAMPFLEURY (1872-89)

Émile BAÜMGART (1890-1)

Édouard GARNIER (1890-1903)

Georges PAPILLON (1903-18)

Maurice SAVREUX (1919-26)
(became factory director)

Georges HAUMONT (1926-42)

Hans HAUG (1942-5)

Henry-Pierre FOUREST (1945-80)

Antoinette FAY-HALLÉ (since 1980)

Select Bibliography

ALBIS, Antoine d' and PREAUD, Tamara, *La Porcelaine de Vincennes*, Paris, 1991.

BOURGEOIS, Émile, *Le Biscuit de Sèvres au XVIIIe siècle*, 2 vols, Paris, 1909.

BRONGNIART, Alexandre, *Traité des arts céramiques...*, 3rd ed. with notes and additions by Alphonse Salvetat, Paris, 1877 (reprinted Paris, 1977).

BRUNET, Marcelle, *Les Marques de Sèvres*, Paris, 1953.

BUMPUS, Bernard, *Pâte sur Pâte: The Art of Ceramic Relief Decoration 1849-1992*, London, 1992.

ERIKSEN, Svend, *Sèvres Porcelain: The James A. de Rothschild Collection at Waddesdon Manor*, Fribourg, 1968.

FAY-HALLE, Antoinette and MUNDT, Barbara, *La Porcelaine européenne au XIXe siècle*, Fribourg, 1982.

LECHEVALLIER-CHEVIGNARD, Georges, *La Manufacture de porcelaine de Sèvres...*, 2 vols, Paris, 1908.

MIDANT, Jean Paul, *Sèvres: La Manufacture au XXe siècle*, Paris, 1992.

SÈVRES: *Elégance du XXe siècle*, Tokyo, 1993.

VERLET, Pierre, GRANDJEAN, Serge and BRUNET, Marcelle, *Sèvres*, Paris, 1953.

Exhibitions

SÈVRES, 1975, *Sèvres Porcelain in the Nineteenth Century*, Musée National de Céramique.

SÈVRES, 1987, *Sèvres Porcelain in the Twentieth Century*, Musée National de Céramique.

SÈVRES, 1989, *New Acquisitions: 1979, 1989*, Musée National de Céramique.